How to Begin
Equine Clicker training:

Improving horse-human communication

Hertha James

Powerword Publications

Muddy Horse Coaching

hertha.james@xtra.co.nz

www.safehorse.info

www.herthamuddyhorse.com

James, Hertha

How to Begin Equine Clicker training: Improving horse-human communication

Some illustrations are taken from video footage so sharpness was sacrificed to capture specific moments.

Dedication

This book is dedicated to all the pioneers of clicker training animals beyond the laboratory, giving them a better chance of understanding the strange things we ask them to do. Film, advertising, zoo, companion, working and pet animals are rapidly joining the clicker training community.

And a special dedication to those northern hemisphere equine clicker trainers who work all through the winter with frozen hands.

Other Books

The following books are also available from Amazon.com as hard copy or as e-books.

They contain lots of background material and specific Training Plans, with free links to YouTube clips.

You can find them any time by putting my name (Hertha James) into the Amazon search engine.

- ***Conversations with Horses***: *An In-depth look at the Signals & Cues between Horses and their Handlers*
- ***Walking with Horses***: *The Eight Leading Positions*
- ***Learn Universal Horse Language***: *No Ropes*
- ***How to Create Good Horse Training Plans***: *The Art of Thin-Slicing*

If you prefer e-books but don't have a Kindle reader, Amazon has a free Kindle reader which can be downloaded to any computer, tablet or smartphone.

Table of Contents

This Book Includes:

Free YouTube Links

Find my YouTube channel with a search for *Hertha Muddyhorse*. Please see the end of the book for a comprehensive list of titles. Relevant video clips are also mentioned throughout the book.

These playlists mainly relate to the ideas in this book:

1. *HorseGym with Boots*: these are numbered. For example, if you would like to view Clip #18, simply put "*#18 HorseGym with Boots*" into the YouTube search engine and it should take you there. Each title starts with its number.
2. *Starting Clicker training*: some older clips when the horses were just learning about Clicker training.
3. *Free-Shaping*: these clips only have names. To find one, click on the playlist name and scroll down to find the title that you want.
4. *Thin-Slicing*: these clips also only have names so please scroll down the list to find the title you want to view.

Eight Thin-Sliced Training Plans

The training plans in the book provide a springboard to make it easier for each handler to write Individual Education Programs for their specific horse or horses.

I can write hundreds of carefully thin-sliced Training Plans based on my experience, but only you can set up an Individual Education Program (IEP) that works for you and your horse.

About the Author

Hertha James began her career as a zoologist working in zoos and as an animal handler on film sets. She then went on to teach high school science and biology for 23 years. She has a lifelong interest in animal behavior, especially horses. Horses have always been a big part of her life.

Hertha is an active participant in international Horse Agility competitions and twice gold medal winner in the World Equine Clicker Games.

She is author of fiction and non-fiction about horsemanship and has written extensive teaching and learning resources. Hertha also produces DVDs and video clips to illustrate the clicker training processes and the fun that can be had when we use reward reinforcement to communicate with our horses.

Snippets

** The purpose of all 'training' or educating of horses is obviously to enlarge their boundaries of understanding, so making them bolder and more reliable in various situations.

** When we slip a halter on a horse and attach a rope, we are changing his whole life. We are putting him 'in uniform'.

** No matter how much we like to 'gloss up' what we do with horses, our intent is for the horse to put his feet where we want them at any particular time.

** It is the most natural thing in the world to want the horse to change so he does what we'd like him to do. However, in reality, it is by changing what we do that gets us closer to the results we want.

** Horses tune in to 'happy vibes' coming from their 'people'. They are equally tuned in to negative, angry, frustrated, fearful or contradictory vibes coming from their 'people'.

** Often people throw a whole lot of new learning at a horse and wonder why he flounders.

** If we are twitchy, the horse will be twitchy. If we are calm and relaxed, the horse has a chance to be calm and relaxed.

** Being with a horse requires our 'risk management radar' to be on at all times.

** Clicker training allows us to shape behavior by allowing the horse to be continually successful.

** Clicker training is not like giving our horse an occasional food treat when we feel like it. It is building a whole new mutual language.

** Nothing will be perfect; learning is a messy business.

Frequent Questions

Q. Do I have to use a mechanical clicker?

No. It's fine to use a tongue click, a special word not used in general speech, any short, clear nonsense word (e.g. ubu) or any special sound like a short whistle. The most important thing is that the sound needs to be consistent.

Q. Where can I get a clicker?

At a pet shop or online looking for 'dog training clicker'

A variety is available. One source is:
http://store.clickertraining.com/clickers.html)

Q. Will I have to click and treat everything my horse does forever?

No. Mainly the click and treat dynamic is used to teach something new and then gradually faded out. For some things, we may use it all the time. It doesn't take long to get into the habit of carrying a few treats with us whenever we are with the horse so even if we are not teaching something new, we can regularly click&treat an uncommonly good effort or an especially nice behavior.

Q. Doesn't hand-feeding cause horses to become biters and nippers?

If the correct method of Clicker training is not understood and carried out thoughtfully, this is possible. Clicker training is a skill the handler needs to learn well and apply consistently in order for the horse to have clarity about what is going on. It can't be done ad hoc or randomly.

Done well, the first thing that the horse learns is that mugging or demanding a treat never works. For every treat given, the horse must first do a requested behavior. Consistent, correct Clicker training eliminates biting and nipping because such behavior never leads to a reward. Instead, the horse focuses on the things you teach that do result in a reward.

Q. Will I be able to use clicker training when riding?

Yes. Once the horse understands the basic voice and touch signals on the ground, we can transfer them to riding. The horse reaches around to retrieve his treat from your hand. Such treat retrieval also helps to keep the horse's attention on you when you ride on green grass outside an arena or a grazed paddock.

Q. How can I teach something like cantering by using clicker training?

We do this by gradually shifting the *click point*. The first *click point* is the actual trot-canter (or walk-canter) depart or transition. When the horse responds confidently and consistently to the 'please canter' signal, the *click point* is gradually moved to after 2-3 strides of canter, 5-6 strides and so on.

Once the horse is confident with canter departs he learns to maintain the gait until the click sounds. Eventually the click&treat is phased out to maybe one at the end of a canter session.

Meanwhile, we can build in an encouragement like 'good' or 'yes' as a *that's right, but keep going* signal. With practice, the flow of the handler's energy in tune with the canter becomes the only *keep going* signal needed. The change in the rider's energy flow when asking for faster or slower gaits will become the main signal for the horse.

Isn't Clicker Training just for tricks?

It's not uncommon for people to think that training tricks is different from 'proper training'. But as recently pointed out by well-known clicker trainer Shawna Karrasch, everything we teach a horse is a 'trick' to him. Little of what we expect a domestic horse to do has any resemblance to the experiences of a free-living horse.

A horse learning to get along with people is forced to learn a new language. Clicker training, done well, takes much of the guesswork out of the equation for the horse. No matter what we want to teach, our click tells the horse, "That's what we want". The treat is a piecework wage for his effort.

Teaching a horse to target our hand with his leg may seem like a trick. However, confident balance on three legs is fundamental to foot care. Everything we teach a domestic horse is a 'trick' to him, since none of it bears any resemblance to a horse's life in the wild.

Exploring Equine Clicker training

What Clicker Training Is Not

Clicker training is not a quick fix for problems. The handler needs to learn the mechanics of treat delivery before heading out to the horse. Then the handler fine-tunes the mechanics of Clicker training by using it to teach simple behaviors.

Sometimes people start with Clicker training but soon give it up again. They never move past the first hurdles to become proficient. What might be the cause of this?

Clicker training opens a whole new realm for handlers and their horses. If a horse has a history of learning forced on him with the use of ropes, small pens, and flailing sticks, he may be excited or bewildered by the prospect of food treats and the idea of having a 'say' in the proceedings.

There will usually be teething problems. The horse's excitement or enthusiasm can show up in ways that make the handler feel uncomfortable and out of control. When the horse is able to express his true self in a pro-active, challenging way, it's often easier for the handler to say, "I tried this a couple of times and it didn't work," than to persist through the inevitable teething problems.

Both the handler and the horse will have teething problems (no pun intended).

A bewildered horse will need lots of time, via very short sessions, to get his head around this new possibility of working for an immediate, tangible reward. I acquired an elderly Thoroughbred who needed nine days of three five-minute sessions per day, until she suddenly saw the connection between the target, the click and the fact that she could pro-actively earn a treat by touching her nose to the target. On the ninth day, it was as if the sun had come up in her eyes.

Becoming adept with this new 'second language' is an exciting business but it does take commitment to learning new information and letting go of information and habits that no longer fit with what we're now striving to do. It can require a significant rearrangement of a person's belief system.

Change is always a challenge. It is especially hard if we are trying to change against the stream of what other people around us do with their horses. It takes a fair amount of belief and stick-ability to persevere to the point of proficiency when we hear unpleasant comments from colleagues. But we may also find some kindred spirits. There are equine clicker training tribes on the Internet. By late 2016, a number of Facebook groups have sprung up to share ideas and give support to people new to clicker training.

The concept and behavioral science behind clicker training is straightforward. It is based on the fact that we are all motivated to do more of whatever makes us feel good or gains us a reward, horses included. However, getting good at the mechanics of clicker training horses and working through the layers of possibilities is not necessarily simple.

Once the handler is proficient and the horse is clicker-savvy, we can use clicker training to build complex chains of behavior. When it is truly adopted, the click&treat dynamic infiltrates every corner of the relationship and becomes the backbone of the horse's Individual Education Programs (IEPs). In other words, clicker training becomes the mainstay of a holistic approach to educating a horse.

What Clicker Training Is

Clicker training is also called the *Mark & Reward System*. We 'mark' the exact behavior we want with the special sound we have chosen and follow the sound with prompt delivery of a food treat that the horse likes.

The special sound is sometimes called a bridging signal. It lets the horse know he has done what we want and it 'bridges' the time gap between the correct behavior and the delivery of the treat. After we click, we pull the treat out of our pocket or pouch and hold it out in a firm, flat hand so the horse can retrieve it easily.

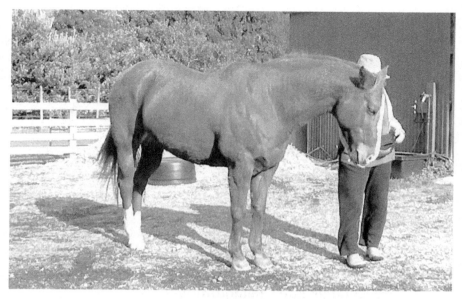

As the horse does what we want, we mark the action with a 'click' and follow up immediately with a small food treat offered away from our body on a flat hand.

People often want to know if they will have to click&treat for everything forever more. The answer is, no. The main use of the click&treat dynamic is to build confidence with new tasks and new expectations. The click&treat is hugely motivating to most horses. If our horse is worried about road traffic, we can click&treat every time a vehicle passes. With repetition, the horse's vehicle anxiety turns into the habit of anticipating a click&treat instead.

Once a horse learns how to solve the relatively simple problems that we set, he tends to show a keenness to solve the next new problem we present. A clip called *Free Shaping Head Lowering* in my *Free*-Shaping playlist shows my horse, Boots, solving a new puzzle. Once a new behavior becomes an established habit, we can phase out the click&treat for that behavior. We may occasionally mark and reward it again if we want to revise it or if the horse makes a special effort or shows staunchness in an unusual situation.

On the other hand, we can choose to click&treat some key routines every time – like paying a piecework wage for good and reliable effort. Some of the things I always click&treat for are:

- come to me out of the paddock
- halter/bridle on
- halter/bridle off
- picking up first foot for cleaning
- after cleaning all four feet
- staying parked on request, click&treat when I return to the horse
- loading into a trailer
- coming to the mounting block
- neck flexion to the right and left after mounting
- immediately after dismounting
- if using mats or nose targets as destinations, upon parking on the mat or touching the nose target.

There are other things such as backing up or keeping calm as a big truck passes us on the road, that I click&treat frequently but not necessarily every time.

The marker signal sound is an integral part of clicker training. The sound does not have to be made with a hand-held mechanical 'clicker'. It can be a special word/sound never used elsewhere (e.g. the nonsense word 'ubu' seemed to work well). One friend simply says, 'Cluck'. Many people use a tongue click. When working across larger distances, such as coming in from a paddock or liberty work, I use a whistle as a recall signal.

Many people who clicker train horses start with a mechanical clicker but once the horse makes the connection between offering a behavior and hearing the marker signal (click), the handler changes the marker to a sound that can be made leaving both hands free. In my experience, horses have no trouble crossing over to a new marker signal as long as it is clear and used consistently.

A mechanical clicker can be helpful at the beginning because it is such a clear, distinct sound. Teaching a horse the connection between our marker sound (i.e. a click) and the food reward is often called 'charging the clicker'.

Some horses are so anxious or sensitive they have a fear reaction to a loud 'click' sound. For such horses, using something like the softer click of a ballpoint pen can be used to begin the training. Or the handler can simply start out with a special word or a tongue click.

Lois Shaw, a Canadian clicker trainer wrote, "Clicker training is a language that both you and your horse are learning to speak together at the same time. Horses do not speak English/French/German/Mandarin. Clicker training creates a neutral language for both horse and human to learn together. The horse can understand you through the clicker and you can understand the horse if you train yourself to listen well."

The main communication between horses is via body language, which is looked at in detail in my book, *Conversations with Horses*.

The Scientific Basis of Clicker training

We all learn from the consequences of our actions. Whenever we do something, we note the consequence. If the consequence is pleasant, we are motivated to **do** that again. If the consequence is unpleasant, we are motivated to **not do** that again.

Signal Pressure

'Signal pressure and the release of that pressure' is the first language of horses and the rest of us. We seek the 'release' of the signal pressure because the release allows us to regain comfort.

Every time someone asks us to do something, we feel the signal pressure. The only way to relieve that pressure is to carry out the request, or say 'no'. Some requests are polite and may be something that we enjoy doing anyway. Other requests make us groan. Signal pressure may come from another person, a pet wanting to be fed or a herd of bulls bellowing to have an electric fence moved along. A pile of dirty dishes is an environmental pressure signal. So is a chocolate bar. Both the dirty dishes and the chocolate can influence our actions.

If we act in a way that removes the signal pressure, we have learned what action will make the pressure go away. Next time we receive the same pressure signal, we'll try that action again. If what we tried did not release the pressure, we have learned one thing that does not work. So we try something else.

Washing the dishes will remove the signal pressure of 'dirty dishes'. Piling the dishes into the sink may reduce the strength of the signal, but it won't remove it. Putting the dirty dishes into the dishwasher will also weaken the signal, but unless we remember to turn on the dishwasher, they will still be dirty in the morning.

All living things have a strong seeking response toward rewarding consequences (e.g. clean dishes or something especially nice to eat). The most basic rewards are what we all need to survive; mainly food, shelter, security, stimulation, mates and a sense of belonging - either to a group or to a landscape.

If our actions not only release the signal pressure, but also result in a reward - something very desirable - we are usually keen to repeat whatever we did so we can earn that reward again. After all, the reason most of us go to work is to provide food and shelter. If we are lucky, our job also provides us with positives like interesting pastimes and a sense of belonging.

Motivation to do something in order to gain a reward is the underlying feature of teaching with positive reinforcement. Good parents use it all the time. Washing the dishes can be followed by a favorite TV program or time on a computer or a piece of chocolate. It is also intrinsically rewarding because it results in clean dishes for next time we want to use them.

Good teachers use positive reinforcement all the time, along with critical assessment. When we receive positive (reward) reinforcement, it makes us glow and often creates the desire to work even harder next time. Horses are the same.

Some horses survive in our strange (to them) human world by living a life of learned helplessness. They comply with just about everything people ask of them. They have learned to suppress their natural instincts and do as they are told because anything else results in increased pressure and pain.

In such an environment, horses who don't learn to suppress their natural instincts, whose independent spirit remains intact, are generally labelled as bothersome, bad or dangerous. They have a history, but often not a happy future.

With clicker training (reward reinforcement), the horse learns to actively seek to repeat the behavior which resulted in the reward. Suddenly the horse can be proactive about initiating a conversation with the handler. He will offer the behaviors we have taught with click&treat in the hope of eliciting a click (marker signal) and the reward that follows.

As well as allowing the horse to be pro-active, clicker training shows horses that it is possible to understand what humans are trying to tell them. Clicker training, done well, starts with what a horse is already able to offer and works forward in small steps or 'slices' to eventually complete a larger complex task.

If we can keep the horse's motivation and confidence each step of the way, he will own the final behavior and carry it out because he understands what we want him to do and because he knows there is something in it for him when he completes the task.

As long as we can keep his confidence intact, the horse usually remains interested in what we are trying to communicate and willingly puts his mind to new puzzles we set him. Rather than shut down or look for escape, he will voluntarily stay with us (mentally and physically) for longer and longer.

Horses who have survived by shutting themselves down into learned helplessness often take a while to make sense of reward reinforcement, because it is so unlike their past dealings with people.

It is a memorable experience to watch a horse like this unfold his personality when he realizes that he is allowed to be proactive. Starting clicker training can also be a scary experience if a horse comes with an inventory of avoidance or aggressive behaviors that have worked for him in the past.

Ways of Using Clicker Training

1. Build 'people confidence' with an anxious horse or one who has little to do with people in the past.
2. Awaken new interests in a horse that is 'shut down'.
3. Create more exciting Individual Education Programs (IEP)s for an *exuberant horse.*
4. Encourage a nervous, *flighty horse* to focus on a task – give him a reason to slow down, think and relax.
5. Give incentive to an *energy-conserving type of horse* to encourage activity.
6. Gently and gradually build confidence with a *quietly anxious horse.*
7. Effectively break our training into tiny steps (slices) that the horse can understand.
8. Teach ourselves to look for the 'smallest try' on the part of the horse and shape all the 'small tries' into the whole behavior we want to develop. As we get better at marking exact *click points* (which are also our pressure release points) we can become clearer and clearer for the horse. He can do less guessing in order to work out what we want. Horse and handler learn this second language together. It becomes a secret language between the two of them.
9. Shows us that learning together never stops. There are always new challenges and puzzles to solve or old ones to improve.
10. Teach ourselves to convert general Training Plans into careful Individual Education Programs (IEP)s and

adjust them as we get feedback from the horse and from ourselves. Eight examples of Training Plans are detailed later in the book.

Designing good training plans for any purpose is explored in detail in my book, *How to Create Good Horse Training Plans: The Art of Thin-Slicing.*

Much can be done with horses using release reinforcement only: that is, applying signal pressure and releasing that pressure when the horse complies. However, to be really successful using only release reinforcement the handler needs:

- a high degree of expertise with reading horse character type
- a very full kit of handling skills to suit each horse character type
- refined intuitive 'feel' to know when the horse is offering a step in the right direction and the ability to immediately release the signal pressure at that moment
- well-honed emotional neutrality (remaining unflappable no matter what happens), which can only come with experience.

It's hard to have the fine-tuned skills mentioned above unless we were apprenticed to a gifted horseman and spent a lifetime (with an open mind) learning from horses themselves.

Clicker training, carefully studied and executed, can help us design and carry out horse education tailored to our particular horse and what we want to do. Training becomes fun for the horse and the handler. Working with reward reinforcement sets up a whole new dimension for the horse and their person.

What Do We Use for Treats?

People use tiny portions of grain, horse nuts, cereal, crackers, bits of dry bread, apple, carrot or celery slices, popcorn (popped), compressed hay pellets, rice cakes — anything the horse likes that can be delivered in very small pieces. It is helpful to experiment with a few things to find out what a particular horse prefers. It is only a 'reward' if the horse really likes it and looks forward to receiving it.

It is often easier if each treat is one discrete piece rather than a handful of loose bits like grain. If the horse knows there is just one item to pick up off the hand, he won't be tempted to scrabble with his lips to check if he has missed something.

Some horses love peppermints. I use small ones as a special treat for an excellent effort and if I want to amplify the importance of what the horse has just done.

A treat pouch with a variety of treats, a clicker on a halyard, a water bottle taped to a stick to use as a nose target, and a dumbbell-like toy for the horse to pick up. Try a variety of treats to see which ones your horse likes best.

Getting Started with Protected Contact

Teaching horses with the mark & reward clicker training system is obviously different from using it to teach dogs or working with dolphins. We can't toss fish into the water to reward the horse, but we can use a halter and rope as a way of 'holding hands'. We can toss treats onto the floor for dogs but that is not useful for horses, although in certain situations we can toss treats into a dish or onto the grass.

The purpose of protected contact is to allow us to step back if the horse gets too enthusiastic. *Rule number one is always to keep ourselves safe.* If we are injured, who is going to look after our horse and continue his education?

The ideal protected contact when we start clicker training is to have the horse on the other side of a safe barrier (not something he can put his foot through). If the horse is used to electric fences and not anxious about standing near them, tape and tread-in posts can work well as long as we remember to *turn them off before the session.* Non-electrified electric fencing materials are super handy because we can set them up to make a training area of any size or shape we want.

We can work over a safe gate or fence or have the horse in a stall. The benefit of having the horse in an area bigger than a stall is that he is free to leave if he wants to, so giving us clearer feedback about his mental and emotional state at the moment.

Protected contact just means being on the other side of a safe fence or gate. It's a good idea to use protected contact when we begin clicker training because it gives us a safe way to find out the horse's reactions when food it introduced into the training. Boots is free to walk away to her paddock if she doesn't want to play clicker games.

If we start with protected contact, we can easily step back if the horse becomes too excited or enthusiastic. Safety is always our first concern, for us and the horse.

If there is no safe barrier option and the horse is calm and comfortable about being tied up with a single rope, we can use tying as protected contact. This is the least ideal option. We need to be careful that the horse is tied high and has a nice drape in the rope so he is not hindered in his responses.

If you work with the clicker while the horse is tied up, be sure that there is a good drape in the rope so that the horse doesn't run into halter pressure when he moves to target your object.

Once the horse is clicker-savvy, it's good to work at liberty with the horse in a roomy enclosure. When we work with a new or exuberant horse at liberty, carrying a dressage whip or a stick&string combination is a logical thing to do. It allows us to have protected contact 'on the move'. It is a safety net in case we need to defend our personal space. We may never need it with some horses, but it is there if a need arises.

Just as we strive to remove anxiety from the horse's training, so we must remove our own anxiety about feeling intimidated by our horse. If we are fearful, the horse will note it right away. Carrying a body extension, held in neutral unless being used to accentuate a signal, is a smart way to make sure that we stay safe. Even the best mannered horse can respond to a sudden or unexpected situation in a way that can hurt the handler or others in the vicinity.

My book, *Learn International Horse Language,* outlines a detailed plan about person and horse learning to feel comfortable with each other at liberty. It is an ideal plan to carry out before doing anything else with a new horse, or to expand a relationship with a horse we already have.

Working at liberty in a roomy area has several advantages.

1. We don't have to manage and manipulate a rope.
2. We can have fun with free-shaping new behaviors (free-shaping is discussed in more detail later in the book with video clip examples).
3. The horse is free to stay and play or leave (which is important feedback for us).
4. There is more space and therefore more scope for a variety of interactions.
5. We can adjust our signals for when the horse is further away.

Background Essentials Before We Head Out to the Horse

Reward reinforcement is also called positive reinforcement because we *add something* (a marker signal and a treat) to the situation.

Release reinforcement is also called negative reinforcement because we put signal pressure on the horse to do something, then we 'release' the signal pressure when the horse complies, so *removing something* from the situation.

The terms 'positive' and 'negative', in the field of animal behavior, are used in a mathematical sense, not in the sense of being 'good' and 'bad'. Both release and reward are highly reinforcing and we inevitably use both all the time.

The only time we don't use release as well as click&treat, is when we are free-shaping to capture a behavior. For free-shaping we simply observe until the desired behavior happens, then 'capture' it with a click&treat. There is no release involved because there is no direct signal pressure involved.

Free-shaping is explained more fully a little further on. My *Free-Shaping Examples* playlist has video clips demonstrating the process in various contexts. This is the link to the shortest clip in the playlist.

Of course, our presence itself, with our clicker and pouch of treats, is a strong environmental signal for the horse. Some clicker trainers advocate only wearing the food pouch or vest when we want clicker work to commence.

Their idea is to take off the food pouch when they've 'finished' with the clicker work. I don't subscribe to this idea for the following reasons.

1. If I've gone to the trouble of making my horse clicker-savvy, I want to be able to use this second language we have developed anytime and anywhere.

2. If there is no click, there is no treat because I base my clicker training on the One Click = One Treat premise. The horse understands this.
3. I expect the horse to carry out behaviors which have become good habits at anytime and anywhere, irrespective of whether or not I have treats on my person.
4. If we don't get into the habit of having treats with us whenever we are with the horse, we can miss some wonderful serendipitous opportunities to capture a unique behavior or to reward an especially strong effort.

Free-Shaping

Clicker training can work with reward reinforcement alone. We quietly, unobtrusively observe, waiting for the horse to do something we like, and click&treat the exact moment of the desired action. For example, we can click&treat each time he lowers his head. Once he's made the connection, we can put a signal (either a gesture or a word or both) on that action, and then we can ask him to lower his head whenever we like.

This is called 'free shaping'. Once he responds correctly to our signal most of the time, we have created a reliable response. Repeated click&treat has built a strong history of reinforcement for that task. It has become a habit. Some people begin clicker training by waiting for the horse to turn his head away from the handler, rewarding that move with click&treat, so showing the horse that mugging does not pay.

If we feed our horse at about the same time every day, he probably comes over expecting to be fed whenever he sees us at a certain time. We have created a reliable or 'conditioned' response because our arrival at that time has been rewarded day after day. It has become a habit.

There are more illustrative clips in my *Free-Shaping Examples* playlist. Getting the horse to touch a target with his nose is an example of free-shaping. We capture a behavior that the horse offered naturally due to his innate curiosity.

Using Signal Pressure for Communication

Free-shaping is fun, but to progress a bit faster with our training we mostly use both release and reward reinforcement when we do clicker training. We apply some sort of signal pressure to cause the horse to do something. When he does, we both release the pressure and click&treat.

The 'click' is the 'bridge' between what the horse has done and the treat he will get for it. It allows us to 'mark' the exact piece of behavior we would like the horse to do, or at least a first approximation of the behavior we would eventually like him to carry out.

The click&treat system causes the horse to focus strongly on finding out what earns the click&treat. He'll start to offer behaviors to earn a treat. It gives him a way to communicate with us. It also allows him ownership of new learning. Soon after starting to learn things with click&treat, horses usually begin to throw behaviors at us, hoping to get the treat vending machine working.

At this point, we could say that the horse is starting to become clicker-savvy. He has a solid understanding of the connection between the click and the forthcoming treat. He understands that he has to offer a behavior to elicit a click&treat. However, we don't want him to randomly offer all or any of the behaviors he has learned.

At this point, it is important to put the new pieces of learning 'on signal' or 'on cue'. Our signals need to clearly communicate what we would like the horse to do. Usually our signal is a touch or a gesture accompanied by a word.

Signals most often arise naturally out of the nature of the task we are teaching. There is a great deal of information about types of signals in my book, *Conversations with Horses*.

For picking things up, I point to the object and ask my horse, Boots, to, "Pick"! At the end of a session she likes to come around with me to pick up all the cones or rags we were using for arena markers.

Once the horse knows the task and the signal, it is important to only click&treat when we have asked for it. Otherwise it would be hard to use cones as arena markers while working with Boots!

I had to put picking up cones 'on signal' so that we can still use cones as arena markers.

The second clip about *free-shaping head lowering* illustrates me trying very hard to put head lowering 'on signal' so that Boots is not forever lowering her head.

Importance of Putting Learned Behaviors 'On Signal'

As mentioned above, a skilled clicker trainer will put learned behaviors 'on signal' or 'on cue' as quickly as possible. We want the horse to wait for our signal before offering the behavior.

A horse throwing his learned behaviors at us might feel like fun at first, but it can become dangerous when the horse choses an inappropriate moment. When I taught Boots to 'spin', it was quite startling when she wanted to show it to me and visitors all the time, while standing right beside us! So, it pays to think carefully about the possible consequences of specific behaviors before we teach them.

You will probably find that the most recent thing you have taught your horse is their favorite move of the moment, since that behavior has lately been strongly rewarded.

It pays to be aware that we can get into trouble, especially if the horse is a confident, imaginative type of horse always checking out his relative place in the social order.

Such horses may perform the learned behavior then 'demand' the treat. It's important to make sure the horse does not develop this option. The treat is always a reward for something you have asked the horse to do. It can't be demanded.

On the other hand, if I sometimes forget to click&treat a behavior that falls into our list of things I always click&treat, Boots makes sure to remind me with a gentle nudge. Once you have a strong relationship and your clicker training repertoire is well established, you will have built up a connection that suits you and a particular horse.

No other training method elicits the enthusiasm and fun that can be had with well-planned and well-executed clicker training. Many horses playing click&treat games never want their sessions to end. Rather than having to worry about 'ending the session on a good note', clicker trainers have to teach an 'end of session' routine to let the horse gently know that the session is finishing.

*'Belly crunching' is one of our favorite 'end of session' games.
It's hard to appreciate in a still photograh, but Boots is using
her abdominal muscles to rock her weight back and lift her
withers up to touch my hand.*

Although the 'marker' does not have to be the sound of a mechanical clicker, using a distinctive mechanical clicker when first teaching something new has the advantage of greater clarity for the horse. It also helps make the handler extremely observant about where to place the current *click point*.

As mentioned earlier, once the horse knows the new behavior, it doesn't seem to matter if a tongue click or a unique, consistent sound/word is used as a bridging signal instead of a mechanical clicker.

Putting each new behavior 'on signal' will gradually reduce the horse's desire to throw the new move at us as soon as he sees us (much like a child dying to show us his new painting).

Usually a horse will have one or two favorite behaviors that he pulls out to see if he can get the vending machine to pay attention. Boots' smile is the one she always tries first.

Keeping the Balance

For most things we teach, we have to also teach a counter-balancing task.

1. If we teach 'head down please', we also need to teach 'head up please'.
2. If we teach 'back up please', we need to teach, 'come forward please'.
3. If we teach targeting a mat with the front feet, we have to teach happily stepping off the mat and walking away from it. Some horses get strongly attached to their mats.
4. If we teach a turn followed by a 'halt', we have to teach a turn followed by a brisk 'walk on please'.
5. If we teach entering a trailer, we need to carefully teach exiting the trailer.
6. If we teach the horse to ground tie, we also need to teach him how to move with a dragging rope so he learns not to step on it and isn't frightened if something happens to make him move dragging his rope.
7. If we teach the horse to come to us when we are playing at liberty, we also need to teach him to move away from us in a way that is fun rather than seen as a punishment. Being sent away to the outskirts of the 'herd' can be seen by horses as a punitive action because it's the most unsafe place to be.
8. If we teach a move or behavior on one side of the horse, we need to teach it again on the other side of the horse. Maybe also from in front of the horse and from behind the horse. This whole topic is explored in detail in my book, *Walking with Horses: The Eight Leading Positions*.

If we don't do these things, the horse will become fixated on one way of doing a task. He'll be determined that he'll always do it this way. In some situations, the power of the click&treat dynamic can work against us rather than for us.

So, for everything we teach, we need to counterbalance it with another task. How much we do of each thing depends on many factors. As we get better at understanding our horse, it will get easier to know when we've done too much of one thing. We'll find it easier and easier to keep a better balance.

Staying Safe and Mugging Behavior

Until we get into the rhythm of using a target, clicking at the right moment and delivering the treat smoothly, it's ideal to keep a safe barrier between ourselves and the horse (protected contact) as described earlier.

If we have no safe barrier, we can tie horse as long as there is good slack in the rope and the horse is relaxed about being tied.

To work safely at liberty, we need a relationship in which the horse willingly backs-up on request (we can teach this with click&treat while using protected contact). Our horse must be polite whenever he enters our personal space or 'bubble'. We need to be equally polite whenever we enter the horse's personal space.

At times when safety is in question, our behavior needs to resemble that of a horse higher in the social order. If we establish our relative position in a horse-like way, our position as CEO is easily accepted by the horse. My book, *Learn Universal Horse Language,* outlines a way to become integrated into our horse's life, playing at liberty, using actions that the horse intuitively understands, and in a way that works to keep both the horse and the handler safe.

Some horses have learned to use their size and strength to intimidate people. Sadly, this is a result of poor handling and poor communication. The horse's behavior can be modified with clicker training by showing him what will be rewarded and what will be ignored or re-directed.

Table manners around food treats need to be taught. Consistency is the key. The horse learns that the treat is only forthcoming if he first does something, and then hears the click. The video clip: *Table Manners for Clicker Training*, in my *Free-Shaping* playlist illustrates the process of developing positive behavior around food treats by rewarding the horse when he turns his head away from the treat pouch and stays facing forward.

To let the horse know when we only want him to stand quietly, clicker trainer Alex Kurland suggests adopting a clear neutral stance by having both hands folded over our belly button. Notice that Bridget also has her energy turned off and she is not looking directly at Smoky.

Developing nice food manners will be harder with some horses than with others. Some horses are naturally polite and gentle with their lips. Others are shark-like or resemble uncontrolled suction machines. If we have one of the shark or suction machine horses, it is a good idea to keep a halter on at first so we can steady his head (and teeth) as he reaches for the treat.

As mentioned earlier, be sure to teach a consistent back-up signal with the horse behind a safe barrier. A consistent back-up sets a good foundation for all future work.

The first session of clicker training with a horse tells us where he is on the 'treat taking behavior' continuum. Getting it politer may need to be the first Individual Education Program (IEP) we write. The ideal is for the treat to be taken delicately from our hand with the tips of the lips.

Dealing with Mugging and Hand-Grabbing

If the horse tends to grab at the treat hand, we can put one hand on the halter and hold his head firmly straight forward as a signal to explain that grabbing is not a desired behavior. We need to help the horse learn that he will get the treat only if he stops grabbing. As much as possible, we want to show him what he should do, not what he shouldn't do.

We have to be careful not to tease him. We need to give him the treat at even the smallest sign of less grabbing. Then we gradually expect more and more politeness as he begins to understand. Ideally, we'd like the horse to wait for our hand to reach his lower lip area before he makes any move to retrieve the treat.

Some horses respond well if we present our hand as a closed fist (with the treat in it), ask them to touch our fist, and then quickly open the hand right under the horse's lower lip.

Some horses respond well if we run our closed fist (with the food in it) downwards along the top of their nose and under the chin before opening our hand.

Both these 'delaying tactics' might make it easier for the horse to tone down his anticipation of the treat. In effect, they become an additional bridging signal between the click and the treat.

Often the mugging behavior fades as our timing gets better, the horse understand the rules better and we are able to keep him busy. If there is too much delay between the click and the treat, some horses can become anxious and mouthier.

If there is too much delay between the repeats of what we are doing, the horse may be tempted fill in the delays with plans of his own.

It's helpful to train in discreet segments of time or number of treats. For example, we can train for 3-5 minutes (or count out a specific number of treats), then have a break by going for a spot of grazing or just relaxing and hanging out, or going for a short walk together around the training area.

Then we can have another short focused session, go for another break, and so on. As mentioned earlier, clicker-savvy horses often don't want their overall session to finish. Training like this is very intense. Our plan has to build in breaks or time doing other familiar activities between short sessions of new focused training.

As much as possible, we want to ignore or redirect unwanted behavior. Jerking or hitting out at a horse is an aggressive act. Horses that are already pushy see such actions as an invitation to escalate the confrontation. They will make a game out of it. It won't get better.

It's important to know how to defend our personal bubble by using our arm to *block* off our space with a quick vertical karate-type movement in the air between us. If we consistently define the boundary of our personal bubble, the horse will learn where it is and be more inclined to keep his distance.

Defining our own boundary is not the same as hitting out toward the horse. Horses understand the difference very clearly. In a sudden stress situation, we can also make our personal bubble bigger by twirling the end of a rope, waving our hat or doing lively jumping jacks.

How Clicker Training Can Influence Our Training

Clicker training teaches both the handler and the horse important things.

1. The horse learns that the click means 'Yes' that's right.
2. The handler learns to look for and click&treat the slightest try in the direction of the desired behavior.

Clicker training allows us to shape behavior by allowing the horse to be continually successful. We do this by putting the following points into place.

1. We start with an end goal clear in our mind.
2. We note what the horse is able to offer already.
3. We work toward our goal through a series of 'successive approximations' which in plain English means gradual tiny changes toward our end goal.
4. Each tiny change becomes the horse's decision. He then 'owns' that change because he understands that he made a good choice because it earned him a click&treat.
5. Unwanted behavior is ignored or re-directed. If we feel unsafe, we return to having a barrier between us and the horse. If the horse's behavior makes us feel unsafe or frustrated, it is essential to go back to the place in our training where both horse and handler feel confident and comfortable. Then work forward again from there. If we feel unsafe or annoyed, the horse will pick up our feeling and also feel unsafe (if he is in anxious mode) or want to leave or take over (if he is in confident mode).
6. It is important to thin-slice end goals into the tiniest clickable moves that we can think of. When we create a written 'Individual Education Program' (IEP) we can make revisions as we go along and learn from experience. We can look back and review how well (or not) a particular horse responded to each slice of the

Program. Being able to look back gives us more feedback so we can adjust the Individual Education Program (IEP).

7. Every change we make is relevant to the horse. If we change something, we have changed a parameter and need to be aware of how the horse might perceive it.

There is a great deal more information about writing training plans and IEPs in my book, *How to Create Good Horse Training Plans: The Art of Thin-Slicing.*

Understanding Parameters

Once we appreciate the sensitivity of horses, we can appreciate how sensitive we need to become about the way we signal our horse. It is often said that, "Everything means something to a horse," or "Nothing means nothing to a horse". That is hard to deny and is probably true for all prey species. We tend to forget, looking at our horses in captivity, that we can take the horse out of the wild, but the wild remains in the horse.

People generally breed those horses with more manageable natures, but a few thousand years is a short time in evolutionary history. A horse is as wired for constant awareness as a squirrel on the lookout for a cat, dog, hawk or snake.

To become an effective teacher and coach for our horse, we need to manage parameters when we are working to create a desired behavior.

A 'parameter' is something that we are keeping constant.

- If we ask for a halt while walking beside the horse's neck, this position is the 'constant' or parameter we have chosen. A click&treat will follow the halt.
- If we then move on to asking the horse to allow us to step in front of him, facing him, after the halt but before the click&treat, we have set a new parameter. We have

behaved differently to create a two-link behavioral chain (halt + wait while I step in front facing you = click&treat).

- If we change standing in front of the halted horse, facing him, to standing in front of him with our back to him, we have introduced a new parameter (change of our body orientation).
- If we step in front of the horse with our back to him and wait five seconds instead of two seconds before the click&treat, we have once again changed a parameter (creating more duration).
- If we step in front of the horse while he is in motion rather than halted, we have changed a parameter.

#45 HorseGym with Boots illustrates the above example of parameter changes.

Whenever we change a parameter, we return to click&treat for less and work our way forward again until the horse can confidently get 10/10 in the new situation.

Horses are super observant of such small changes. They can often be thrown by something which may seem insignificant to us. It is so easy to lose their relaxation and willingness if we proceed too fast or ask for too much too soon. By 'thrown', I mean that the horse has a loss of confidence. It may be only a small loss quickly remedied. But it could also be a major loss causing the horse to look away or want to move his feet to escape the situation. If he can't escape, he may mentally shut down instead.

The solution is always to back up in the Individual Education Program (IEP) to a point where confidence remains, and work forward again from that point. There is more information about creating IEPs later in the book.

People who are really good with horses have learned the following particulars.

- They have become aware of their own body language.
- They can read the horse's body language – not just the big things, but the small nuances particular to each individual horse.
- They recognize a variety of innate horse character types which are not much different from what we observe in humans. They develop strategies that work best for each type. Horse character types are explored in more detail in Chapter 3 of my book, *How to Create Good Horse Training Plans: The Art of Thin-Slicing.*
- They expect horses that are not 'shut down' to act differently in different locations, different situations and with different handlers.
- They allow adjustment time when the environment changes.
- They appreciate that tame horses see us as part of their herd and form very close bonds with favorite people, just as they do with favorite horse friends.
- They understand that the sheer size of horses means that there is always an element of possible unintended physical injury caused by the horse's startle response.
- They understand that to safely be part of a horse's in-group means maintaining a standing in the group social order at least a step higher than the horse.

As we gain experience with horse sensitivity, our own body orientation and the signals we are using, we will get better and better. We will become more aware of which parameters we are setting and when we change them. This is an integral part of 'thin-slicing' large tasks into their smallest teachable parts. There is more detail about 'thin-slicing' later in the book.

Rules Work in Both Directions

We can think of parameters as the rules of the game. It is up to us to teach the horse the rules of the game we want to play with him. Equally, it is up to us to stay true to the rules.

The horse can only become as reliable as we are reliable in our teaching and everyday handling.

All the things we want to do with horses entail having control of where the horse puts or keeps his feet. We can then add other things to go with this 'foot control': things like being connected to person with a rope, wearing a saddle, carrying a rider, specific body flexions and particular ways of moving his feet.

To teach the rules of the game fairly, the handler needs to be aware of these things:

- the thin-slices probably needed to teach the overall task to this particular horse
- how little or how much the horse already understands about the task
- gaps in the handler's training skills
- how the handler is orientating his body in relation to the horse (at all times)
- the consistency (or not) of his signals
- how good the timing of his release plus click&treat is
- how good and consistent his rope handling skills are
- how good and consistent the handling of his body extensions (including rope/reins) is
- how good he is at using his breathing and core body energy to show intent and relaxation.

The horse can only be as smooth as the handler is smooth. The horse can only learn as smoothly as we can teach smoothly. Becoming aware of when we change parameters (i.e. when unconscious changes become conscious) is a big step forward as we develop our horse handling skills.

The Nitti-Gritty of Treat Delivery

Most clicker trainers deliver the treat in a flat open hand. But there are alternatives. Some establishments have a 'no hand feeding' rule. The solution is to tie a small, flattish, plastic bowl (Frisbees have been used successfully) around the wrist or attached to a belt. After the click, hold the bowl, put in the treat and offer the bowl to the horse.

It's also possible to toss the treat into a feed dish after the click. This works as long as the training involves the horse standing still or moving in a very small area. The dish could be on the ground or up on a stand so it is easier to toss in the treat.

Training Plan One: Empowering a Shy or Timid Horse

Using a familiar feed dish can help if we are working with a shy or timid horse, or one unused to humans. We can use *free-shaping to capture the behavior* of taking a treat from the feed bucket. Here is the thin-slicing for a possible Training Plan.

1. Place the feed dish between us and the horse. The horse will tell us how close we can be without causing him to move further away.
2. Wait in a relaxed manner (not staring at the horse) until the horse looks at the feed dish – click and quietly move to the feed dish and toss in a treat. Then immediately move twice as far away as our former position, giving the horse the personal bubble size he needs to feel safe enough to approach the feed dish. It's good if the treat makes a sound when it hits the dish.
3. Wait for the horse to retrieve the treat. If he can't do it, move further away or go do something else and come back later. He'll usually check the dish while you are away.
4. Approach the feed dish until the horse moves away (if he hasn't already). As soon as the horse stops, stop as

well. Watch for him to look at the feed dish – click and quietly move to the food dish and toss in a treat, then glide away again to a distance that respects the horse's current personal bubble. While watching the horse, we need to be careful not to stare directly at him, but to observe him discretely with our peripheral vision. He will begin to connect the click with the food treat about to be tossed into his dish.

5. Repeat 10-20 times or as long as the horse shows interest.

6. Each horse is different. Some horses easily shrink the size of the space they need to feel safe and soon take a step toward the dish. Others will find it harder to build confidence.

7. It's possible to do this procedure on the other side of a fence from the horse. It is protected contact for us, but it can also make the horse feel safer from his point of view.

8. Gradually we can shift the 'click point' to wait for a step toward the food dish, then sniffing the food dish. At the same time, we may be able to gradually decrease the distance we have to move away before the horse will retrieve the treat.

9. Eventually we can sit in a chair with the bucket near us, then right beside us, then on our lap and the horse will come to retrieve his treat from the bucket.

10. From there, we can introduce our hand into the bucket and get him used to the idea that he can pick food off our hand.

11. Eventually we can dispense with the bucket.

Smooth Treat Delivery before Heading out to our Horse!

Find a friend or family member with whom you can practice the click and smooth treat delivery. Have them stand in as your horse and get them to touch a target which you hold out when you want a response. Coins or wrapped candy or bits of cardboard make good 'treats'.

It's a big help to the horse if we learn the motor skills with another person before heading out to our horse.

Organize a pocket or a waist/bum bag that easily lets your hand in and out to get the treats. Smooth treat handling is really important when we first start with the horse.

Hold the target out in front of you. Click the instant your helper touches the target. Move the target out of sight behind your back and reach for the treat in your pocket or pouch. Pull out the treat and offer it to your pretend horse in a firm, flat, hand at the end of your fully extended arm.

After the click, move the target out of sight and present the treat in a firm, flat hand well away from your body.

Focus on:

- the timing of the click at the moment the person (horse) touches the target
- moving of the target behind your back as you reach for the treat
- stretching your arm as far as you can to offer the treat
- holding your hand totally flat (palm up) and very firm so the person (horse) can take the treat as if from a steady, solid plate.

Here are the individual steps to the process:

1. Have your hand ready on the clicker (if using a clicker).
2. Present the target a little bit away from the person (horse), so s/he has to reach out to touch it.
3. Wait for the person (horse) to touch the target with their hand (be patient). Ignore any unwanted behavior.
4. The instant they touch it, click or say your chosen word/sound.
5. Drop the target down and behind your body to take it out of play.
6. Reach into your pocket/pouch for the treat.
7. Extend your arm fully to give the treat.
8. Stretch the treat hand out totally flat so it is like a flat plate with the treat on it.
9. Hold your arm and hand very firm so your pretend horse or your real horse can't push it down. If they tend to push down, push upwards with equal pressure.
10. Begin again with #1.
11. If the person pretending to be your horse (or your horse) tries to mug you for a treat, turn your shoulder or move your body/pouch out of reach. The treat can only be earned by touching the target.
12. Short sessions (about 3-5 minutes) with breaks in-between allow your brain & muscle memory to absorb the technique, especially the finer points of timing.

When it all feels smooth, have a turn being the horse so you can feel what it is like from the horse's point of view. Then you are ready to head out to the horse.

Starting with Your Horse

Reminders

If your horse lunges for the treat

Some horses are always polite, others not so! Be safe. For the first sessions have a barrier between you and the horse so you can move back out of range if necessary (or have the horse tied if that is your only option).

Be sure that the horse is not hungry. I always train after the horse has been grazing or has eaten hay.

The ideal training situation is when the horse can see his herd mates, but they are not able to interfere. This may not always be possible. Sometimes we just have to make the best deal out of the facilities that we have.

Until you have a good idea about how your horse will react to the click&treat dynamic, be safe by working on the other side of a fence, gate or stall guard. If none of those are available, having the horse tied up is an option. Note the drape in Boots' rope so she won't hit the end of it when she reaches for the target. For regular tying up, the rope would be shorter.

If things are not going smoothly, check out your 'treat delivery' method. *Common difficulties are*:

- Does it take too long to get your hand into and out of your pocket or pouch?
- Do you move your hand toward your treats BEFORE you've clicked? This can cause major problems because the horse will be watching your hand rather than focused on what you are wanting him to learn. It's best to recognize and stop this before it turns into a habit.

Be sure to only feed treats if they have been earned *and you have clicked*. Always ask the horse *to do something* before giving a treat. For example, ask him to take a step backwards. If you click by mistake, give the horse the treat. He shouldn't pay for the handler's mistake.

Hold your treat hand where you want the horse's nose to be, not where he sticks his nose. If the horse tends to shuffle toward you, hold the treat toward his chest so he has to shift backwards to retrieve it. We can use the same procedure to teach a back-up signal while the horse is still behind a barrier.

If he lunges for the treat, first try the backing up technique outlined in the paragraph above. He will form the habit of expecting to move back to retrieve the treat. Alternately, put a halter on and hold the side of it after the click, so you have some control of where he puts his mouth.

With a horse that is not timid, you can also use a sharp verbal inhibitor signal – loud sharp "uh" (as in 'up') as a warning that the current behavior is not what you are after. However, using your body orientation and where you place your hand with the treat is more effective and useful.

As mentioned earlier, it can help to run the closed treat hand down the horse's nose from above, ask him to target your fist, then open the hand under his chin so he can retrieve the treat. With consistency and patience on the handler's part, extra keen treat retrieval behavior usually improves over time. The more consistent we are, the faster it will improve.

Smoky, who features in some of the pictures and video clips, almost jumped out of his skin with excitement and anticipation when we started using clicker training. We used all the suggestions above to keep our hands safe. Eventually, as reward reinforcement became a regular part of his day, his treat taking became more refined.

Free-Shaping Polite Table Manners

At some point, early in the clicker training process, we'll use free-shaping to teach the horse that it's best to keep his head looking forward rather than turn it to us in anticipation of the treat.

It's easiest if there is no barrier between you and the horse so you can easily stand shoulder-to-shoulder with him. However, you can line him up beside you on the other side of a gate or fence into the shoulder-to-shoulder position, or have him tied up.

Some trainers use this as their very first lesson to teach the horse the connection between the click and the treat. I prefer to use targeting as the first lesson, because it gives the horse something logical to do (i.e. touch his nose to the target object to earn a click&treat), rather than asking him to resist his natural impulse to move his nose toward the food.

Free-shaping is simply being in the horse's vicinity in a relaxed manner and waiting for the horse to do something that we would like him to do. We click as the action happens and deliver a treat. Horses quickly learn what they need to do to earn the treat, and willingly do it again.

To teach politeness at the halt, we stand quietly shoulder-to-shoulder beside the horse (who may be behind a barrier), hand on the clicker (if using one), and wait for him to turn his head away from us or keep it facing forward for a second or two: click&treat.

If he nuzzles our pocket or pouch, we ignore it, turn slightly away from him, or move away a step or two. Whenever he moves his head away from the food source, or keeps his head facing forward, we click&treat. We start with a click&treat for one second of keeping his head straight or turned away.

In essence, we are capturing and marking the moment his head turns away from us (or if it remains facing forward) with the timing of our click. We are rewarding the 'facing forward' or movement away with the click&treat. The video clip illustrating this process is in my *Free-Shaping* playlist, called *Table Manners for Clicker Training*.

Gradually, in one-second increments, we increase the time we can stand together politely at the halt. This process is called 'building duration'.

When I stand relaxed with my hands together, resting in front of my treat pouch or on my belly button, Boots knows the task is to stand quietly facing forward. As with all training, the keys are consistency and frequent opportunity to practice.

It is fun to 'capture' desirable behaviors like this, without using signal pressure to initiate a movement. The horse seems to have more of a feeling that he is teaching us when to 'click&treat', which is strongly motivating for him. It gives him an opportunity to start a conversation.

Triple Treats

Once the horse understands the dynamics of the click&treat game we can introduce the idea of 'triple treats' for an especially brilliant effort. The technique is illustrated in *#16 HorseGym with Boots.*

We ask the horse to target our outstretched fist, click & give him the treat with our other hand. Then we repeat the process two more times in quick succession so that he earns three 'easy' treats in a row by simply targeting our non-feeding hand made into a fist and held up so he has to stretch his neck to reach it.

The Triple Treat functions as a break during a focused training session or as a reward for a special effort.

The 'triple treat' creates a mini 'time out' from the concentrated work the horse and handler are doing. It's a small interlude to let our brains relax. The horse soon understands that it is a reward for a good effort, especially if we add happy verbal praise as we do it. We can also use it to end a session.

Giving Meaning to the Click Using a Target

Training Plan Two: Capturing the Targeting Behavior

As already mentioned, in order to begin, we have to teach the horse the meaning of the 'click' or marker word/sound that we are going to use. This is sometimes called 'charging the clicker'. A good way to do this is to use a target object that we hold out for the horse to touch with his nose.

A target could be a plastic bottle taped to the end of a stick, a cone, anything safe for the horse to touch with his nose and easy for us to hold. A target on the end of a stick is handy for later, when we want the horse to move and follow the target.

Plastic bottles are good because we can accumulate lots of them and hang them around our environment so we can walk with the horse from fixed target to fixed target. It makes an ideal way to teach the horse to lead willingly or to ride out confidently. *#84 HorseGym with Boots* illustrates some of this.

To begin, we use free-shaping to 'capture' this brand-new behavior. We're teaching the horse that there is a connection between the 'click' marker sound and a treat. Remember, we don't have to use a mechanical clicker. A tongue click or a special unique word or sound can work well, as long as it is consistent.

Target on a Stick — Part A

The final goal, after lots of sessions, is for the horse to happily move his feet to follow the target. *#2 HorseGym with Boots* demonstrates the various stages of the process.

First Session

1. Count about 20 treats into your pocket/pouch. Have a few spares handy in case you want finish the session with a jackpot. Jackpots can be a special generous portion of treats put in a dish or on the ground, or they can come in the form of a 'triple treat'.
2. Hold the target near his nose, but don't thrust it **at** him.

3.   *Wait* until he touches even a whisker to it — click/treat and move the target out of sight behind you. This will encourage his attention to the target when you present it again for the next repeat.

When you offer the target, place it where it is easy for the horse to touch with his nose, but make sure that the horse closes the gap to make the touch. Don't thrust it at his nose.

4.   Reach for the treat and deliver it away from your body by holding your hand out straight and rotating your shoulder to create a solid platform with your totally flat hand.

After the click, move the target behind your body and offer the treat in a flat hand, well away from your body.

5. Put your hand on the clicker (if using one) ready to click again.
6. If he is unsure about touching the target, gently and slowly move the target back and forth near his nose until it just 'happens' to touch a whisker: Click&treat, removing the target out of play as you do so.
7. Then hold out the target again. Keep it easy for him to touch for your early sessions, until you can see that he really 'gets it'.
8. Repeat about 19 times or work for about three minutes. Ignore unwanted behavior. Try to stop on a HIGH, when you've just had a really good response. A jackpot or a 'triple treat' can be a nice conclusion to a session.

Lots of short sessions (about 20 treats or 3-5 minutes) work best. Keep all your *parameters* the same until you get 10/10 confident repeats in a row, every time, over about three consecutive sessions. As you gain experience, you will get a feel for:

- when it's time to move on to the next challenge
- when it's wise to spend a bit longer on the present challenge
- when to return to a previous step.

Quick Reminder about Parameters

A parameter is something that you are keeping constant, e.g. holding the target always near the horse's nose at the beginning is the 'constant' or parameter you have chosen.

- If you change to holding the target up higher, that is a new parameter.
- Holding the target down low is another new parameter.
- Setting the target down on the ground instead of holding it in your hand is changing a parameter.
- Using a different target is changing a parameter.
- If you change where you are standing in relation to the horse, you've changed a parameter.
- If the horse is confidently taking three steps to reach the target, and you begin to ask for five steps, you have changed a parameter.
- If you move from outside the enclose to being inside the horse's enclosure, you have changed a parameter.

Whenever you change a parameter, you have changed your *click point*. Return to clicking for 'less' and work your way forward again until the horse can confidently get 10/10 in the new situation.

Horses are super observant of such small changes, and can often be thrown by them if we proceed too fast or ask for too much too soon.

Criteria and *Click Points*

Whenever we change the criteria for what we will click&treat, we are changing a parameter. As mentioned above, each changed criterion or new parameter means a rethink about your *click points*.

Target on a Stick — Part B — *the next sessions*

1. Once the horse is confidently touching the target held near his nose and seldom loses focus, gradually change the position of the target to make it more challenging for him. Chose **one** of: higher, lower, to the right, to the left. Teach each of these one at a time.

Rather than presenting the target straight ahead, I'm asking Boots to turn her head to her left.

2. When he can confidently reach in each direction, start to mix them up.
3. When he moves his neck to follow the target willingly and with interest, ask him to move a step to the right or the left to reach it. Stay with one direction until he is superb at it, then teach the other direction.

4. At some point, ask him to reach well over the barrier to touch the target, then offer the treat close to his chest so that he has to take a step back to retrieve the treat. You may have to adjust the height of your barrier so you can reach across it comfortably. If that's not possible, you could change to having the horse tied up if you don't yet feel ready to work at liberty.

5. When he smoothly steps back to get his treat, add gesture and voice signals as he backs. Expecting to take a step back to get his treat is a good habit for the horse to develop. It's also a major safety feature to have in place.

6. When he happily moves one step to follow the target, gradually build up more steps. You can still be on the other side of a barrier to teach this.

7. When you feel safe, work without the barrier. If you ever feel unsafe, return to using a barrier.

8. When you change any parameter, begin by clicking for *less* until confidence is regained. Then gradually start to *withhold the click* to get a tiny bit more of what you want.

9. If he gets confused, always be ready to back-track to the place where he can be continuously successful. This is the key to over-all success and rapid progress. If he gives up because it's too hard or too confusing, you have lost his willingness. Stop on a high. Resist that urge to do it again to see if you can do it again.

10. Get creative until he'll happily follow the target (over things, between things, into things like a trailer or a trailer simulation).

Boots is doing a weave pattern by following the target which is a milk bottle taped to the end of a plastic garden stake.

The great thing about starting clicker training by using a target is that when we finish the session, we can put the target away.

#3-#7 *HorseGym with Boots* video clips show how we can expand the use of nose targets.

#9-#14 *HorseGym with Boots* illustrate teaching and using foot targets.

Generalizing Target Work

Once we have the horse happily following a target, we can use it to expand our activities.

1.   We can carry a small, familiar target and when the horse comes across something that worries him, take it out and ask him to target it as a way of relaxing his mind. It allows him to focus on something familiar.

2.   Once the horse knows the voice 'target' signal, we can ask him to 'target' general objects we come across on a walk or out riding.

3.   We can hang targets around our training area and walk/trot between them. Because the horse has a destination with something in it for him (click&treat at each one) we can establish a lovely habit of moving along beside us. Eventually we can phase out the

targets, but the polite leading habit will remain. *#84 HorseGym with Boots* demonstrates moving from target to target at liberty.

4. We can move between fixed targets to help a horse become confident about being ridden, or to create more willingness in a horse who has become reluctant under saddle (as long as we are aware that such reluctance could be due to physical pain issues that may need investigating).

5. For a horse worried about leaving home, we can hang targets along our route so that he has something familiar to focus on rather than worry about going further away from home. We can gradually put the targets further apart and have fewer of them. Once the confidence to 'go out' is established, the targets won't be needed. For a horse who is very anxious about leaving home, the targets can be set out in a semi-circle that takes the horse away from home and returns him to home.

6. These ideas work equally well with ground work and riding.

7. To develop work on a circle, we can use a target on a stick and set up a circle pattern to walk around. We can make a round pen with temporary materials and walk inside the round pen while the horse moves around the outside.

8. A lot of this work can be done at liberty if we have a safe enclosed area. The horse can develop his lateral flexion on the circle unimpeded by a rope. If he tends to fall in over the shoulder, the round pen barrier will help to counterbalance that tendency, helping to strengthen his muscles on both sides of his body.

9. We can teach liberty free-jumping using two people with targets either side of the jump. Start with just teaching

the 'send' to the other person's target in close proximity, then gradually increase the distance and eventually introduce a rail between the two people, then a low jump and so on.

10. If working alone, we can set up a rail or jump with a target on either side and send the horse across to touch the target, click when he does and follow him across to deliver the treat.

11. Following on from the above idea, we can set up four targets at the corners of a square and teach the horse to move from target to target. Add a rail between the targets and eventually work up to low jumps, and so on. We start with a smallish square and gradually make it bigger.

Shaping New Behaviors

Thin-Slicing Explained

When we see a horse performing a finished behavior, it is often tempting to try it ourselves with our horse, by repeating it as we saw it. But that is not how it works.

When we want to train something new, the first step is to experiment a bit to see what the horse can offer already, in relation to the new goal we'd like to achieve. This will give us an idea of where our Individual Education Program (IEP) needs to start. We want to base it on foundation training with which the horse is already confident.

It is also a good way to find any 'training holes' that we need to fill before we enthusiastically head toward setting a new challenge for the horse.

Once we have a starting point, we can begin to write our IEP by thin-slicing the overall task.

The first step of thin-slicing is a brainstorm to dissect the complete task into its smallest teachable components. Then we have to organize these components or 'slices' into an order that we think will make sense to our horse. This possible order of slices becomes the basis of our Individual Education Program (IEP). What makes sense to any particular horse will depend on:

- his innate character type
- his previous life experiences
- the degree of communication that already exists between the horse and the handler
- frequency of the training sessions
- how comfortable the horse feels in the training environment
- effective use of objects and obstacles to make it easier for the horse to understand our intent.

An IEP is always a 'work in progress' and usually we go back and tweak it many times. Sometimes we throw the whole thing out and start again. Each time we work with the horse, we get additional feedback from the horse and from our own reactions and responses.

Thin-slicing means carefully checking (and re-checking) that the horse is comfortable and confident with each tiny slice of the process before we move on. It pays to remember that the *process* of teaching does not look like the finished product.

We have to balance the need to build confidence at each tiny step with the need to move on when we should, so the horse doesn't get bored. It's never easy to walk the fine line between moving too fast and going to slow.

It all becomes easier as experience:

- gives us a deeper understanding of a particular horse's character type
- improves our reading of the nuances of horse body language
- makes us more aware of our own body language and the messages we are giving

- improves our thin-slicing, so creating better Individual Education Programs.

<u>Training Plan Three</u>: Willing Haltering

One horse may learn to sniff his halter (click&treat) and put his head in the halter (click&treat) in less than two minutes. Another horse may take a week of short sessions to just approach a halter lying on the ground or hanging on a fence. His Individual Education Program (IEP) might be sliced to include click&treat for each of the following slices. We stay with each slice until the horse is ho-hum with it.

1. The horse looks toward the halter.
2. The horse steps even the tiniest step toward the halter (Note that with very anxious horses, we can 'sweeten' ideas like this by putting the halter beside a familiar feed dish or a pile of hay. In other words, we use complementary motivating environmental signals to help initiate a response that we can click&treat).
3. He confidently touches his nose to the halter.

By slicing the overall goal small enough, we can gradually create a positive association with a halter.

4. As 3. when the halter is in different places.
5. As 3. when the halter is in a person's hand.
6. Confidence when the halter in the hand is moved
7. Confidence with allowing himself to be touched on the neck with the halter.
8. Confident with the halter touching his face.
9. Confident with the handler putting one arm up over his neck.

At this point we may want to teach the horse to be proactive about putting his nose into the halter. We can begin with something like a small hula hoop to take the place of the halter because it is easier to hold.

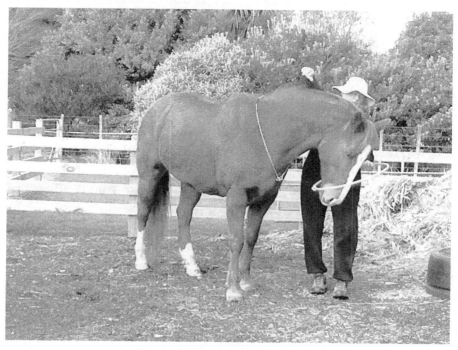

It's easier to hold a small hoop when we first teach the horse to drop his head into an opening. This will eventually be the nosepiece of a halter. I'm also building confidence about having my right arm lying across the horse's neck.

Eventually we can click&treat the following slices.

10. When the horse moves his head toward the hoop.
11. When the horse moves his head to the left and drops his nose into the hoop.
12. When we can lift the hoop up toward his eyes and take it away again.
13. When we can lift the hoop up over his eyes and take it away again.
14. When we can lift the hoop past his ears and take it away again.
15. When we can lift the hoop over his ears and lay it on his neck and take it away again.
16. When we can do the steps above with a halter rather than a hoop.
17. When we can slip on the halter and lay the halter strap behind his ears and take it away again.
18. When we can hold the halter strap in position for longer.
19. When we can do up the halter strap and undo it again and take the halter off.
20. When we can put on the halter and leave it on for a short time.
21. When we can put the halter on and take it off two or three times in a row.

#65 HorseGym with Boots illustrates the procedure.

We start with teaching the most basic prerequisite behavior. When the horse clearly understands our request for that behavior (which could take a couple of minutes or up to many, many sessions), we add in the next 'slice' of behavior that will lead to our ultimate goal. We can and should move on when:

• the way we give the signal is consistent and clear (e.g. put our right arm over his neck and hold the halter open so the horse can put his nose into it)

66

- the horse presents the behavior we want 99% of the time (when we hold the halter open, he puts his nose into it)
- the horse does not add in any unwanted behavior (e.g. running away first, chewing on the halter).

If the situation becomes confused, it is usually because we have not cut the whole task into thin enough slices. Although we have an ultimate goal, the ultimate goal is not where we put our attention. Our attention is directed at each 'slice' or mini-skill.

Mastering these one by one and linking them together, as the horse is ready, will seamlessly bring us to our ultimate goal – the whole task that we thin-sliced at the beginning is performed smoothly with one click&treat at the end.

When confusion arises (in either the horse or the handler or both), it is essential to return to previous work until we find the 'slice' at which both the horse and the handler can regain their confidence. Then we simply work forward again from that point. This is Mastery Learning. Each small part is mastered before moving on to the next part.

When we do reach our ultimate goal, it will be underpinned with a solid foundation of understanding. The horse will understand what we are asking him to do. We will understand how we got the horse confident enough to achieve our goal.

This is quite different from the thin, one dimensional veneer of performance training often put on horses by a professional trainer where time equals money.

Although our goal is to build up progressively more complex tasks, it is important to remember that teaching anything with a good foundation is not the work of one or two training sessions. We don't drill the first slice so that we can add in the second slice. We provide regular and frequent opportunities for learning, without any of the pressure of drilling.

The last section of this book includes further thin-sliced training plans that can be used as starting points to create Individual Education Programs (IEPs) for a specific horse. It is often easier to adapt something already written than to start from scratch with a blank page.

Preventing Drilling: the Rule of Three

It's good to have at least three different things we'd like to do in a training session, along with (or part of) warming up and warming down exercises. A nice combination might be:

1. something that we already know, to keep it fresh
2. something to improve or practice
3. something new we are working on.

To keep a session lively and interesting, we can look for a good effort at one of these, then move to one of the other activities or have a short break. Then we can choose to return to the first activity or move on to another of our other three activities.

In other words, our plan is to visit each of the three activities three times in a session, in the order that fits best at the time.

I like to stay with each activity until there is a tiny bit of improvement over last time. However, if the horse's first effort is close to perfect, I don't ask for it again right away. We celebrate instead and move on to something else.

If a horse does something correctly and we ask him to do it again to practice, the horse can misunderstand our meaning and think he wasn't correct enough the first time, which is why we are asking him to do it again right away.

He may either try some experimentation to see if he can figure out what we want, or he can lose his confidence and his enthusiasm to keep trying. Many short separate sessions on a particular task usually yield a better result.

People short of time, who consistently work for a few minutes a day on one thing, often find that the short, consistent repeats, highly and frequently reinforced, make that task a reliable part of the horse's repertoire.

So, in summary, as we head out to the horse, it helps to have three tasks to work with. Stay with each to reach a small improvement or get a good response if the horse already knows the task.

Return to each task three times during a session. Of course, we can break this rule any time to suit what the horse needs, but it is a good starting point when we plan a session.

Creating Training Plans and IEPs

Only the handler can create an Individual Education Program (IEP) for a particular horse. But we can look at more examples of Training Plans that can be turned into IEPs. Already we've looked at Training Plans for:

- treat delivery
- capturing the targeting behavior
- haltering a shy horse.

Ideally, we want to teach in a way that keeps the horse being continually successful. We want the horse to maintain his confidence with each part of the teaching/learning process. Clicker training is a system that underlies a person's whole relationship with the horse.

Horses always do the best they can in the situation they are in. As we get better at understanding their perception of reality, our training will be more empathetic. We will take note of what the horse is actually doing, plus the emotions than run alongside the actions. The horse's responses or reactions tell us where our focus should be at each precise moment.

As a coach for our horse, we are always on the lookout for:

- increasing fluency as a new task is learned
- relaxation and calmness
- balance throughout the task
- positive energy brought to the task.

Any and all of these are worthy of a click&treat.

As well as the reliable food reward, many horses begin to enjoy the attention and the mental stimulation of the puzzles we help them unravel. We can enrich their environment and alleviate, to a small degree, the endless boredom of their life in captivity.

The Training Plans presented here can be used as a springboard to create Individual Education Programs (IEPs) that suit your immediate purpose for a particular horse. Soon you will be outlining your own Training Plans and developing your IEPs from them.

This topic is so interesting it caused me to write a whole book: *How to Create Good Horse Training Plans: The Art of Thin-Slicing.*

A bit of terminology:

Click Point refers to the specific movement or behavior we are looking for to reinforce with a 'click&treat'. We need to be clear in our mind what will earn a click&treat before we begin to communicate with the horse.

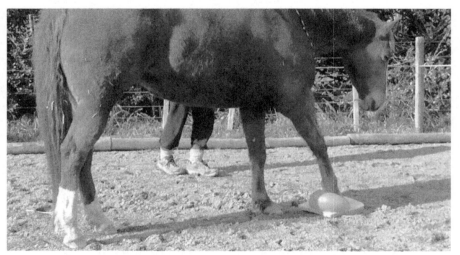

If the horse knows about bursting balloons, my click point would be the moment she squarely lands her foot on the balloon to burst it. If she was first learning the task, my click point would be the first lift of her foot near the balloon.

Teaching Phase is when we first introduce our horse to a new task and give him ample opportunity to practice it over many short sessions and eventually in different places.

When stepping confidently through a solid curtain was a new task for Horse Agility, I set up the situation so it was easy for Boots to work it out by making it the only entrance into her shelter which we use every day.

During the _teaching phase,_ we are usually also in our own teaching/learning phase, as we experiment with signals until we and the horse reach an agreement that makes sense to both of us. Most signals evolve quite naturally out of the training process.

Fluency is when our signals are consistent and smooth. We no longer have to exaggerate our signals for the horse to understand our intent. The signal pressure has become information the horse knows how to deal with. The signal is now a two-way communication and can become quite subtle.

Fluency arises when we do something often enough so that our signal to the horse can become very small. Bridget asks Boots to walk along using a tiny tap behind the withers.

<u>Consolidation and Generalization</u> are achieved when our horse can confidently carry out our requests in new locations and new situations.

In most cases, we teach new tasks in a place where the horse is comfortable and able to relax. If we plan to take the horse away from home, either walking, riding or traveling, consolidation and generalization become extremely important.

We have to give the horse ample chances to practice and use his new skill. Then we need to generalize it to new places and novel situations by calmly and gradually setting up more demanding exposures. Often horses are literally thrown in at the deep end of a new situation which takes them way beyond their comfort zone. Hence the tendency for many people to adopt tools of tighter and more painful constraint in order to 'control' their horses.

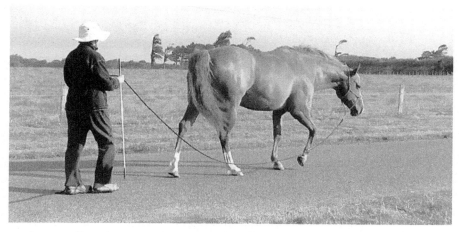

Generalization: Once Boots was confident at home with me walking behind her in Leading Position Six, we generalized the skill by practicing out on the road.

<u>Maintenance</u> means that we review a task on a regular basis if it is not something we do every day as part of management.

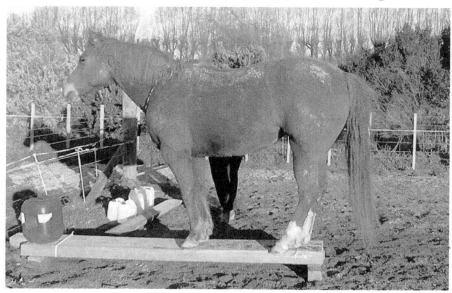

Maintenance: Balancing on a small platform is not something we do regularly, so if I want to maintain it in our repertoire I have to occasionally set up a practice session.

How We Introduce Something New is Critical

Ideally, we consider the following points before we start.

- We have thin-sliced the task into its smallest teachable parts and have an idea of where the early *click points* will be.
- We have organized a training environment where the horse is able to relax. Ideally, he can see his herd mates but they are not able to interfere.
- We have thought about which part of the horse's body we need to influence, and we've planned possible signal(s) to use (energy levels, body posture, body position, gesture, touch, words, strong intent). My book, *Conversations with Horses, An In-Depth Look at Signs and Signals between Horses and their Handlers*, details this topic.
- The environment is set up to make it as easy as possible for the horse to understand what we want (use of a 'lane' or a corner; where we place the mat target or a nose target; use of barriers on the far side of the horse; where we position our body).

Ideally, we make the desired behavior easy for the horse to do, and what we don't want harder for him to do. Setting up the training environment to achieve this means we are already halfway there.

If, instead, the horse learns evasive moves during our first fumbling with a new task, our education program has suddenly become more complex and longer. A bit of thoughtful planning can make things much easier for us and for the horse.

Ideally, we first try out our ideas with another person standing in as the horse. Or we can trial our process on a more experienced, forgiving horse. That allows us to eliminate some of the early trial and error in relation to our positioning and body language.

It allows us to be clearer for the horse when we first introduce something new, rather than confuse him because we have not yet worked out a smooth way to proceed.

The first step is always to make sure the horse is relaxed and in a learning frame of mind. If something has brought up his adrenalin, we do calming procedures or something active until he's used up the adrenalin and can return to relaxation. If he is uninterested, we need to make ourselves and our treats more interesting. Maybe the horse is tired due to the weather or other activities.

Or we wait to start the new thing in a later session. If he gets tense during a training session, we must return to relaxation before continuing.

We start teaching each slice of the whole task with *click points* determined by what the horse is able to offer already. As both horse and handler get smooth with each tiny slice, we gradually chain the slices together and shift the *click point* until the whole task can be achieved with one *click point* at the end.

When we begin teaching something new, we start by finding a beginning *click point*. For some things, this may be a very rough approximation of the final goal behavior, e.g. just a tiny drop of the head when we begin to teach head lowering right to the ground.

This is illustrated in the first of two *Head Lowering* video clips in my *Free-Shaping Examples* playlist.

We gradually shift the *click point* toward closer and closer approximations of what we want until we achieve the goal behavior.

Good timing of the click allows the horse to become more and more accurate.

When teaching something new, the focus of click&treat is on the new learning, but we can still click&treat good execution of things the horse already knows.

Consolidation of New Learning & Developing Fluidity

The *Consolidation Phase* begins when the horse generally understands our intent, our signals and usually responds willingly with the move we want.

At this point, we can keep up interest and enthusiasm by providing an extra click&treat whenever any part of the task is done really well.

To put a new task into long-term memory (for horses and for people) it needs to be practiced *at least* 9 or 10 sessions in a row; ideally over 9 or 10 days in a row. Some tasks will take longer, depending on their complexity.

If we can't have a session every day, we need to accept that it will take longer to build a new behavior solidly. Keeping a written record becomes essential.

How many 'repeats' we should do during one session is hard to pin down because it depends so much on:

- what we are teaching
- the character type, age and history of the horse
- the skill of the handler
- the nature of the handler-horse relationship.

For some tasks, a rule of thumb might be three practice repeats in a row, unless the first one is perfect and calls for a major celebration. Clicker-savvy horses are usually keen to work until you decide to stop, but even a keen horse can use a short break after 10 repeats of learning something new.

If the horse is in the initial learning stage, looking for a tiny improvement over last time is a good *click point*, followed by celebration and doing something relaxing. During the whole training session, we could return to the 'new learning' task three times, in-between doing other things.

Once I started clicker training, it was hard for me to go back to training in a way that does not incorporate it.

Clicker training is nothing like giving our horse an occasional food treat when we feel like it. It is building a whole new mutual language.

Here are five more Training Plans. Each one could be used as a basis for creating an Individual Education Plan for a specific horse.

Five More Training Plans

Training Plan Four: Using Mats as Foot Targets

What to use for Foot Targets?

- Doormats — these tend to be heavy enough not to blow away too easily. Rubber ones can live outside.
- Pieces of carpet — remnants or ask at a carpet store for a book of their outdated samples.
- Pieces of foam rubber — light to carry around.
- Flattened cardboard boxes — inexpensive but may wear out (make sure there are no staples); or use any stiff piece of cardboard (might be slippery).
- Square, round or rectangular pieces of board — stay put in wind and give a good clunk so the horse gets clear feedback that his foot or feet are 'on there' (ensure the board doesn't tip up if the horse stands on one end).
- Tarpaulins — large enough for parking all four feet or folded to make a smaller surface.
- Leftover linoleum pieces or soft tiles — but use the back side if the shiny side is slippery.
- Hula hoop sized hoops, but made from hose joined with doweling so that if the horse has a panic attack, the hoop will come apart.

- Eventually, plastic carton lids for parking one foot — easy to carry around.
- Old electric blankets — tend to be heavy enough to stay put in a breeze. Large enough to park all four feet; old sheets or blankets (weigh down corners if breezy).

Boots demonstrates a variety of foot targets in *#10 HorseGym with Boots*.

Teaching about foot targets is fun and can be used in all the ways we used nose-touch targets plus more. We can free shape 'standing on the mat' at liberty.

It's also fine to do 'guided free-shaping', with the horse wearing halter and rope. The idea is to use direct rope/halter pressure as little as possible. The idea is to encourage the horse to do his own exploration.

If we don't have a safe enclosed work area, using a halter and rope may be our only option. A light long rope or lunge line will allow us to give the horse more freedom of movement. We have to become adept at 'rope management', i.e. letting it out and reeling in so that we can keep it out of the horse's way but not restrict his exploration.

Free-shaping, as described earlier in the book, is when we set up a situation for the horse to explore in his own time. We simply wait, quietly observing in a relaxed manner, until the horse makes his own approach to the mat.

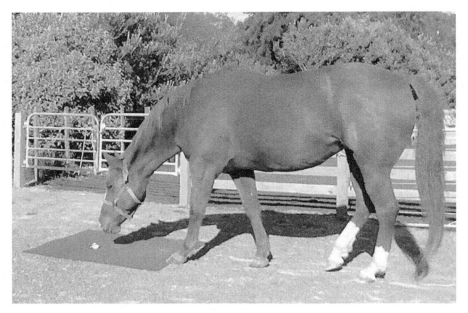

To free-shape the horse to step on a mat, we set it up and allow the horse to approach in his own time. To make the mat more alluring, we can put a treat on it.

Free-Shaping the Foot Target

With the horse able to watch, but ideally behind a gate, tied up or held by someone else, put the chosen foot target in the middle of a safe enclosed area where your horse can be turned loose to explore. This is the ideal, note the comment above if the horse has to be on halter and lead.

1. Make sure the horse is in a relaxed, inquisitive, learning frame of mind. It's easiest if his herd buddies can be in view but not able to interfere.
2. Have clicker (if using one) and treats ready before you turn the horse loose. A chair to relax in can be handy. This is not something we rush.
3. Turn the horse loose (or allow him to explore on a loose rope). Hopefully he will investigate the 'new thing' which is the mat. If he is a relaxed horse and has been

watching curiously while you put the mat out, this is likely to happen.

4. As soon as a whisker or foot touches the mat, click&treat. This could occur right away or you may have to sit and relax for a while until it happens.

5. If the horse doesn't approach the mat, find a beginning point by clicking for body orientation toward the mat or looking toward the mat or the slightest approach toward it. Go to him to deliver the treat, then move away and return to casually observing.

6. If the horse paws the mat, ignore the pawing but click&treat the instant the pawing stops. If the horse was very reluctant to approach the mat, you can click the first 'pawing' movement as his 'first touch'. Maybe click&treat again the instant he stops pawing. As he becomes more confident with the mat, click&treat only when he stops pawing. See #14 *HorseGym with Boots*.

7. Once the horse is happy to target the mat (with nose or foot or both) pick up the mat and move it a short distance away, then back off and relax or sit down, but be ready to click&treat the moment the horse touches the mat again.

8. An alternative to moving the mat is to have the halter on the horse. After each click&treat, clip on a lead rope and ask him to back away or walk forward away from the mat, then unclip the rope so he is at liberty again.

9. After unclipping, move away, relax and observe until he's returned to the mat for another click&treat. If your horse readily walks with you at liberty, you can ask him to walk away without the halter and lead. Be sure to also click&treat after he has willingly left the mat with you.

10. If the horse is reluctant to go near the mat, it can help to jump up and down on it to 'kill' it while the horse is

watching. Then leave it and return to relaxing/sitting down to await the horse's next approach to the mat.

11. Repeat until the horse realizes that going to the mat will result in a click&treat. He may be touching it only with his nose or he may put a foot on it (or both). Click&treat for either one at this point.

12. If the horse is extremely nervous of the mat and reluctant to approach it even after you have jumped on it to 'kill' it, try putting a familiar food bucket on it (or near it) and toss in a strip of carrot or other treat. Click just as he reaches into the bucket. He's finding his own treat.

13. Eventually put the bucket out of sight but lay a treat on the mat. Click just as he reaches for the treat. Stay with this until the horse approaches the mat willingly, at which point you can begin to click for touching the mat and return to delivering the treat via your pocket or pouch.

We can stop a session at any time. If the horse indicates that 'he's had enough for now', we should always stop.

If the horse remains keen and interested, a good place to finish the first session is when the horse shows he's 'got it' by reliably going to the mat each time you move it or, if you walked him away, he eagerly returns to it.

If you needed to use a bucket and/or a treat lying on the mat to gain the horse's interest, a good place to stop is when you can see (and feel) that the horse has gained even the smallest bit of confidence to work through the puzzle you have set him.

The horse will reflect on what happened and next time you bring out the mat, he will usually know exactly what to do. When you consistently get two front feet halted on the mat, *you have free-shaped a brand-new behavior.*

Teaching via free-shaping means that 'going to the mat' has become the horse's idea. When he learns uninfluenced by direct signal pressure, the horse seems to have stronger *ownership* of the new behavior. Just like we feel proud ownership of our good ideas.

From the horse's perspective, we have given him a voice in the conversation.

We say, "Look, I'm moving the mat over here."

The horse says, "Look, I'm going to go stand on the mat and I'm pretty sure you're going to click and come over to give me a treat."

We are having a conversation: we understand each other. And it can all be done without the interference of physical pushing or pulling.

Uses of Foot Targets

Moving from Point A to Point B

As with nose targets, mats are superb in getting the horse to move with us willingly from A to B because there is a destination and purpose that the horse can understand. We can be doing groundwork (including long-reining) or riding.

Going from A to B comes in many guises:

1. Basic movement between any two places, any distance apart, in a straight line, a meandering line or weave patterns. #12 HorseGym with Boots shows how mats can be used to create a behavior chain.

2. A mat in a corner is a clear starting point for teaching a horse to back up confidently because there is no option to go forward and less option to swing the hind end away. Training Plan Five looks at teaching the back-up.

3. If we are teaching or refining a skill such as walking or trotting over poles (or jumping), a mat set out well beyond the poles or jump will give the horse incentive and purpose to complete the obstacle and head for the mat. Once the skill is strongly established and has become a habit, the mat becomes unnecessary.

4. We can put a mat at either end of a specific moving exercise: e.g. a series of objects to weave through. As the horse reaches the mat at each end of the weave, a click&treat gives him a mini-break from the concentration of the exercise.

5. A circle of six or eight markers with a mat on the perimeter can help teach a lovely, smooth 'Walk On' and an elegant 'Halt' to both energy-conserving horses (some people call them 'lazy') and horses that tend to jump out of their skin (some people call them 'spirited'). The handler walks around the outside of the markers and the horse walks on the outside of the handler. Ask for a halt each time you reach the mat: click&treat.

6. That sets us up with a new opportunity to practice our 'walk on' signals to move around the circle again to the mat for our next 'halt': click&treat. Be sure to work on both sides of the horse.

7. A mat in the middle of a circle of markers can be a used as a starting point. From the middle, walk out and around a chosen marker and back to the mat. This move encourages the horse to engage his hind end so he can efficiently move around the marker to return to the mat. Spirited horses will slow down to reach the mat. Energy-conserving horses will speed up to reach the mat. We can vary the diameter of the circle of markers to suit the size of the horse and his level of flexibility.

8. A mat in the center of two objects set to create a 'figure eight' obstacle, encourages the horse to work his right side and his left side equally in order to elegantly return to the mat each time for a click&treat.

Detail about this sort of work is available in my book, *How to Create Good Horse Training Plans: The Art of Thin-Slicing.*

Groundwork or Riding

Mats work equally well with groundwork and riding. The horse will form the habit of going forward at our suggestion because there is always a 'result' in the form of a destination which makes sense to him. Eventually, this habit of following our suggestion will be so strong that targets are a no longer necessary (unless we pull them out to teach something new).

The horse will be comfortable moving with us. We can put in a *click point* when he does something well. We celebrate the good things and ignore, redirect or quietly work through the less desirable behaviors until we reach another piece of excellence to click&treat.

Training Plan Five: A Confident Back-Up

A mat placed in a corner is a great spot to begin teaching a horse about confident backing-up on request. We lead him to the mat and he earns a click&treat for standing on the mat. Then he is asked politely to back off the mat, and earns a click&treat for backing.

We start with one step back and work up to as many steps as we want. We are using something he already knows — to target the mat — and adding a new thing he needs to learn — backing-up willingly in response to our signal.

#27 HorseGym with Boots demonstrates the process.

#7 HorseGym with Boots is another demonstration with Smoky.

A twelve-minute clip called *Backing Up* in my *Thin-Slicing* playlist gives a bit more detail with Smoky.

Importance of a Willing Back-Up

1. Teach safety behavior: the horse yields backwards, out of our space, in response to specific signals.
2. Teach safe negotiation of gates, into and out of stalls or small pens.

3. Teach confident trailer unloading. Many horses are reluctant to get into a trailer because they can't see how they will get out again.
4. Practice getting out of tricky and awkward places such as wash-bays, lanes and tight spots on a trail.
5. Practice confident backing down slopes (and ramps) and up slopes.
6. Every smooth downward transition uses the 'back up' muscles, which means that 'backing' gymnastic exercises help strengthen the horse's hind end.
7. Teaching confidence with having the butt against a barrier, as will be necessary in a trailer or truck.
8. Teaching the horse to seek with his hind legs like he will have to do to step out of a trailer backwards.

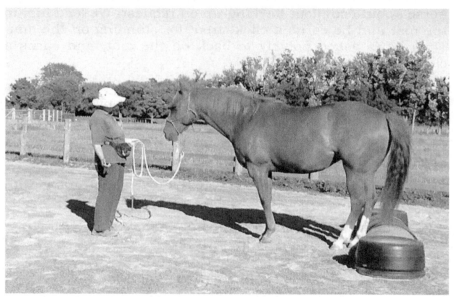

Precision backing to teach the horse to seek with his hind feet. My right hand is gesturing to ask Boots to move her left hind leg a tiny bit more so it touches the half barrel.

Set it Up to Make it as Easy as Possible

1. Use a safe fence or barrier on the far side of the horse. This will help keep him straight. We don't want to create the habit of swinging the hindquarters sideways instead of backing up straight. Avoid strung wire or wire mesh fences that the horse could step back into causing injury. If no fence is suitable, use raised rails or barrels. If the horse is confident working around them, electric fencing materials are useful to set up any arrangement of fence-lines, pens, or lanes.

2. Sometimes a structured lane is useful. To see lanes in action, check out *#39-#40 HorseGym with Boots*. *Training Plan Eight* later in the book is about using lanes. The horse walks into the lane to target the mat and the handler walks along the outside of the lane. A lane helps prevent the horse from learning that swinging his hind end sideways is an option. It is good to build the 'backing straight' habit from the very beginning if possible.

3. Carry a body extension (stick, stick&string, whip, swishy, reed, wand) held in neutral but ready for use (with as little energy as possible but as much energy as needed to be effective) to quietly accentuate your signals as necessary. You may not need it, but it is there to provide clarity for the horse about what you want. Clarity of communication and confidence go hand-in-hand.

4. Have a second mat to which you can direct the horse between teaching sequences. This gives you both a relaxation spot for short mental breaks away from the new learning situation.

5. A 6' or 8' lead rope is good for this type of work. It's easier if there is no rope dragging around your feet or looped in your hand.

6. Start on the horse's 'easier' side. But be sure to teach everything on both sides. Switching sides consistently develops a much better balanced horse and handler.

Two terms explained:

Outside hand refers to the hand furthest away from the horse.

Inside hand refers to the hand nearest the horse.

These obviously change depending on which side of the horse you are on, and whether you are shoulder-to-shoulder with the horse, i.e. both facing the same direction, or you are facing the horse.

Process: the 'In-Hand Back-Up'

1. As mentioned earlier, this is illustrated in *#27 HorseGym with Boots* and the clip called *Backing Up* in my *Thin-Slicing Examples* playlist.
2. Put a familiar mat in a safe corner you've set up for the session. Starting in a corner (or maybe a lane: see *Training Plan Example Eight* later in the book) limits the horse's options about how to respond to your 'back-up' signals. Give the horse opportunity to get familiar and comfortable in the corner by entering and exiting the corner without any backing-up.
3. Your position is beside the horse's head/neck holding the rope in the hand nearest the horse. Handler walks on the open side of the corner set-up.
4. Walk the horse into the corner and ask him to target the mat in the corner: click&treat.
5. Smoothly pivot 180 degrees so you face the horse but are a bit to one side of him.
6. ***In the moment **before** you pivot...***
7. Gently reach across and run your 'outside hand', up the rope to a point of contact to which the horse will respond. At first, this may be right up to the snap on

the halter, or if using a rope halter, even beyond the snap to hold the bottom of the halter, so you can give the horse a very direct backwards *feel* on the halter. As you pivot to face the horse what *was* your 'outside hand' becomes your 'inside hand' — the one nearest the horse.

Bridget (with a great look of concentration because this was her first time doing this) has reached across with her outside hand and is about to run it up the rope toward the halter as she pivots to face Smoky. Once she has pivoted, this hand will become her inside hand.

8. Then simply keep a 'hold' tension on the halter. This causes the horse slight discomfort by making him feel unbalanced. We want him to work out that he can regain his balance by shifting backwards. Our *click point* is the moment he thinks of moving back. Because he's in a corner, it makes sense to him to step backwards to regain his balance.

I've pivoted to face Boots and you can see my right hand is poised to slide up the rope toward the halter. Because Boots already knows this well, I seldom need to do more than turn toward her and use the intent in my body language. She is already in the act of stepping backwards.

9. To begin with, click&treat (and simultaneously release your 'hold') at the horse's smallest inclination to shift his weight back. Then slide up the rope again and 'hold' a bit longer to get a whole step. As he begins to understand, eventually ask for two steps, then three steps and so on.

10. After two or three click&treats for backing-up, ask the horse to step forward to target the mat again: click&treat. Build up a little rhythm of movement: back up = click&treat. Forward to mat = click&treat. Back up = click&treat, and so on. After about 3 of these, walk to your second mat or special grazing spot for relaxation time.

11. Gradually, over many sessions, ask for more steps back until the horse willingly offers as many as you like.
12. Move away from the corner and use just a fence on the far side.
13. Move away from the fence and use just a low raised rail on the far side.
14. Repeat with just a ground rail along the far side.
15. Check to see how well the horse can back with this signal (you facing him and a bit to one side) out in the open. If you lose straightness at any point, return to using a fence or rail on the far side.
16. Be sure to teach all the slices on both sides of the horse.

Process: Generalizations

Look for interesting places to expand your horse's 'backing-up' repertoire with this leading position (facing horse and a bit to one side):

- Set up trailer simulations to go into and back out
- Create or find safe 'tight spots' to walk into and back out of
- Back a figure 8
- Back a short weave pattern
- Back down slopes (start with gradual slopes, progress to steeper ones)
- Back up slopes
- Back onto and off unusual surfaces
- Back over rails
- Back between rails
- Back into lanes with sides of varying heights
- Back to put butt against safe barriers (to prepare for the butt bar being put up in a trailer)

Training Plan Six: Parking with Duration and Distance

Purpose:

It's handy if we can leave our horse 'parked' while we do things around him or at a distance from him. We want to build his confidence to stay parked when we move away from him.

Staying parked is the foundation of tying up confidently, grooming, hosing, massage, foot care, vet inspection, vaccination, traveling in a vehicle, saddling or harnessing, unsaddling/unharnessing, mounting and dismounting.

We can use clicker training to teach all sorts of behaviors that are done at the halt.

Each new successful behavior at the 'halt' will build a bit more confidence.

It's essential to remember that it's not natural for a horse to stand still when there is commotion around him. 'Staying Parked' in strange situations is totally a learned response. We are asking the horse to be 'actively' inactive, which is a high-level skill.

Video clip *#20 HorseGym with Boots* highlights the importance of teaching standing still as a specific skill.

#8 HorseGym with Boots looks at increasing parking duration.

#15 HorseGym with Boots look at increasing the distance you can move away while the horse stays parked.

Materials:

1. Horse outfitted with halter and rope at least 10' (~3m) long.
2. Horse's buddies in view, if possible, but not able to interfere.
3. A clear decision about what we will use for our 'stay' gesture and voice signals. Clicker, if we are using one. It's helpful to use a mechanical clicker when we are

teaching something new. This task is a good one for actually using a mechanical clicker because we are not doing much with our hands.

4. Horse in a familiar area, calm and in a learning frame of mind. If he is not in a learning frame of mind, there is no point trying to teach him anything new. If the horse has an adrenalin rush, we need to do active things with him to work off the adrenalin before moving on to our teaching/learning task. Once his adrenalin has worn off, options are to take him for a walk and a spot of grazing to get him back into connection with us, or to return him to his paddock and come back another time.

Method:

1. Make sure the horse is confident using a foot target (see *Training Plan Four: Using Mats as Foot Targets*).

2. Put a familiar mat in a place you know the horse usually finds comfortable. Make sure there is enough space to allow you to occasionally walk/trot a circuit away from the mat for a relaxation break between the training segments.

3. Park the horse on the mat for one or two seconds. Click&treat.

4. Walk a loop or circuit together and return to the mat. Ask the horse to park using body language, gesture, breath-out and verbal signal; click&treat.

5. Quietly move one step away. Keep a nice 'smile'/drape in the rope. You want zero pressure on the halter. Wait a few seconds. *Return to the horse* and click as you reach him. Give him his treat. *We want him to stay on the mat to get his treat.*

6. Repeat 5. And 6. above until the horse is totally ho-hum about you moving away staying away for a while and return to him.

7. At this point, the focus of training is our distance away from the horse. We can keep the time element short when we start teaching distance. The time element will increase naturally as we move further and further away. Later, if we want, we can build more time on top of distance.

8. Before moving further away, teach him to stay parked while you move one step away on his left side, on his right side and while standing in front of him. Remember, horses can't focus with both eyes on something close and directly in front, so if you stand within a meter of his nose, he may move his head so he can see you with one eye.

9. When going one step away is smooth and relaxed, take two steps away, pause, *then return to the horse before you click.* Then deliver the treat. This part is important because the main thing we are teaching is to **stay parked**. The horse learns that he needs to stay where he is and that we will return before we click and we will deliver the treat to him, no matter how far away we go while he remains parked.

10. Do all three positions (left, right, in front) at each distance. You may find that the horse is fine with one eye, and totally unhappy when you move away in the other eye. That is valuable feedback and simply tells you that the horse needs lots more time to build his confidence in that eye. This will improve once you are in the habit of teaching everything on both sides of the horse.

11. As you get further away, put the rope over his neck or back. If he knows about being ground–tied, drop the end of the rope on the ground. If the horse moves off the mat, treat it as unimportant. Simply pick up the rope, calmly walk a loop, return to the mat and go back to whatever distance/time span the horse can manage at the moment.

12. Energy conserving horses usually find it easier to 'stay put'. Extroverted horses generally have a harder time keeping their feet still. For them, this can become a valuable lesson in emotional control.

13. If the horse gets into high energy mode, we need to either use up that adrenalin before resuming any parking lessons, or change the lesson topic for that session.

14. If our session includes high energy training, parking can be a nice way to relax between energetic tasks and/or to finish the session.

Play the parking game on a regular basis until you get the distance that fits in with what you do with your horse. Our horses (energy conserving types) will stay parked, up to 40 meters across the arena from us, for a long time while we go to get different gear, replenish treats or re-arrange the arena furniture.

Generalizations:

1. Set up, or find, different places to put the mat and ask your horse to park. Be sure to stay within his comfort zone, as this skill is hard to build and very easy to lose if we suddenly expect more than the horse is able to give. His body language will show us the boundaries of his comfort zone.

2. You can develop a dropped lead rope instead of the mat as a place to park. Try using a simple dropped rope for a parking signal when the horse is at liberty. Chapter 8

of my book, *How to Create Good Horse Training Plans* has a detailed Training Plan about teaching a horse to ground tie. The process is illustrated in #72 and #73 HorseGym with Boots.

3. Play with parking at liberty using a gesture and word.
4. Counterbalance the parking skill with recalls.
5. Experiment with asking him to stay parked while you momentarily move out of sight behind a tree, shed, horse trailer or crouch down behind barrels. When we put a horse in a trailer, much of the anxiety he feels is because we (his herd of the moment) suddenly disappear. Horses are wired to stay within sight of their herd. Losing visual contact in the wild can be a death sentence. We can take the horse out of the wild, but we can't take the genetic programming that ensures survival in the wild out of the horse.
6. Gradually, in one-second increments, increase the time out of view. If he moves, try not to make him feel wrong. Pick up the rope and walk a short circuit back to the mat and start again with a shorter time interval that he can manage.

#18 *HorseGym with Boots* demonstrates teaching parking when the handler goes out of sight.

Training Plan Seven: Rope Relaxation

Rope Relaxation is one of the most important life skills we can teach our horse. When we put on a rope, we are curtailing one of the horse's most important freedoms — the freedom to move his feet away from a situation he is unsure about. We are in effect putting him 'in uniform' and have expectations about how we want him to behave.

If we watch a horse at liberty confronted with a new or scary object, he will come as close as he dares, then retreat, turn and re-assess. If nothing scary has happened, he will approach again, this time a bit closer as his curiosity kicks in. Depending on his age, nature and education, he will repeat this 'retreat and approach' until he has decided whether this new thing is harmless or not.

For a horse living in the wild, using up energy unnecessarily is a bad idea. Outrunning predators and laying down fat to survive summer drought and winter cold are more important. Mares need their energy to feed their foals. It's therefore extremely important that horses have the ability to quickly relax once something unusual is seen to be harmless.

When we put a rope on a horse, we are restricting a very basic survival instinct. It makes sense, therefore, to take the time and trouble to carefully introduce the horse to ropes and get him comfortable with all the shapes and forms ropes can take.

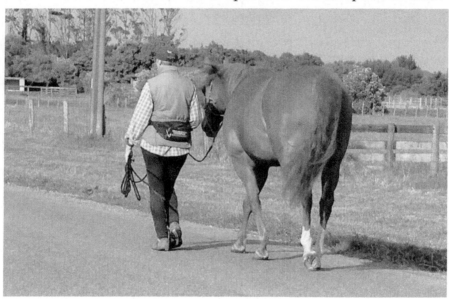

To be connected to a person with a rope is a totally foreign concept for horses.

People have long put on halter and rope and tied a horse to a study post with the idea of letting him fight until he works out the physics of the situation. Often the horse exhausts himself with panic-induced actions. Often there is damage to the neck vertebrae with repercussions through the rest of his body, maybe for life.

Physical problems often go unnoticed by people because horses do their best to hide disabilities. This is because obvious disabilities are direct signals to predators, telling them which herd member to single out for a meal.

Panic-inducing rope experiences mean the horse has been let down by his handler emotionally, physically and intellectually. Since haltering is often one of the first training experiences a horse has, fright-filled rope experiences do not set him up for confidence regarding anything else that people might want to do with him.

While it is important that we teach our horse to tie up, we should not need to tie him up for general care and husbandry. (See *Training Plan Six, Parking.*)

The rope is ideally introduced as an extension of the handler's body — a way of 'holding hands' so that pressure signals can be applied carefully and accurately. It takes quite a shift in most people's thinking to see the rope as a hand-holding communication tool instead of a piece of equipment to stop their horse running away or to drag the horse from A to B.

For a horse totally unfamiliar with ropes, or to re-educate a horse with rope anxiety, we can begin by using a coiled rope as a nose target for a click&treat game while the horse is at liberty in a safe enclosed area (larger than a stall). We might start with the coiled rope lying on the ground, then hanging on a fence before playing with it in our hand.

Once the horse happily targets the coiled rope, we can change the parameters, one at a time, to click&treat when the coiled rope:

- gently touches his neck and withers area
- gently moves on his body until it can be rubbed everywhere.

Then we can change the parameter and *click point* to gently tossing the end of a soft rope to touch various parts of his body.

In some cases, it makes sense to use a second rope to do this, rather than the end of the lead rope attached to the horse. We'd stay with each body part until touching there is ho-hum.

#22 HorseGym with Boots demonstrates some ways we can help the horse become ho-hum with ropes

#35 HorseGym with Boots adds a few more points, from the 2-minute mark, about not only ropes, but also other body extensions we may use.

#60 HorseGym with Boots also looks at Rope Calmness.

We want the horse comfortable with rope touch to:

- his neck, both sides
- his withers, both sides
- along his back, both sides
- down his front legs
- on his chest
- under his belly
- behind, across his tail
- over his rump, both sides.

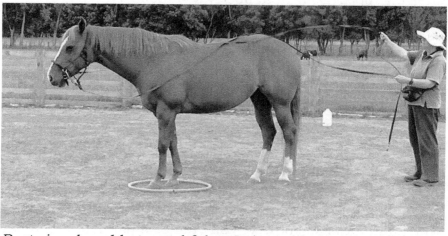

Boots is relaxed but watchful as I play with the long reins from behind. We use the hoop in the same way as a mat. It is a place to park until further notice.

During all of this, the handler needs to maintain a relaxed manner watching to click&treat any sign of relaxation in the horse; such as:

- lowered head
- breathing out
- blowing out
- shaking the neck and head
- licking and chewing
- relaxed lower lip
- softer ears
- softer eyes
- cocked hind leg.

Once the horse is comfortable with the end of a rope gently tossed all over his body, do the same with a stick&string combination or the flexible end of a lunging whip. Tossing it over should resemble another horse's tail; like horses standing head to tail swishing the flies off each other.

Once the horse is comfortable with the end of a rope or string moving all around his legs, it is time to get him used to dragging ropes. Doing it at liberty in a roomy enclosed area, as shown in clip # 22 mentioned above is a lot of fun.

With the horse at liberty in a safe, roomy area, walk around dragging a long rope.

Our *click points* could be:

- when the horse shows the slightest interest in the dragging rope
- when he put his nose toward the end of the rope
- when we stop, the horse puts his nose on the rope
- if he stands still (relaxed, maybe parked on a mat) while we walk around him dragging the rope.

When all that is smooth, we can change a parameter by tying a plastic bottle to the end of the rope and go through the four steps again, still at liberty. The bottle may cause a higher level of excitement and play, or a fear response which will be interesting to work through.

The next parameter change is to have the horse on a halter and lead and ask him to walk beside us while we drag a long rope behind us. Have the dragged rope about 20 feet (7 meters) long. Click&treat for any increasing signs of relaxation while we:

- walk a large circle to the right
- walk a large circle to the left
- halt and pause the dragging rope
- walk on and re-activate the dragging rope

We have achieved this task once the horse is confident seeing the dragging rope behind him out of either eye and walks along calmly in either direction with the handler on either side of the horse.

Generalizations

1. Drag the rope & container on different surfaces such as sand, asphalt, concrete. The noise of the container on different surfaces will create a new challenge. Go back and work through the same *click points* as above.
2. Tie different things to the end of the rope and walk around together pulling them.
3. Ask the horse to stay parked while you pull things on a rope past him or around him. Pebbles in a plastic bottle add more noise to the task.
4. This next idea is a high-level task so only do it if the horse is truly confident with everything else. Be sure to keep yourself safe. Tie a rope to the horse's halter and let him get used to dragging it around and untangling himself when he gets tangled up. Have a second lead rope on him so you are 'holding hands' and can help him out if he gets into difficulty. We want him to think

his way through the puzzle, not get so worried that he has to react rather than respond.

5. Introduce long-reining. My book, *Walking with Horses: The Eight Leading Positions*, looks at long-reining, illustrated by clips *#57-#64 HorseGym with Boots*.

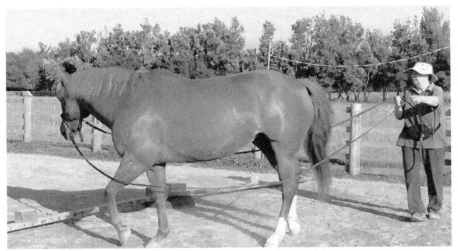

Long-reining is a skill we can use to guide the horse from behind long before we ever want to ride him.

Training Plan Eight: Using Lanes

Lanes are incredibly useful for teaching horses to confidently:

- walk between things on the ground
- walk through narrow spaces
- walk into a closed off space, halt and remain parked in a relaxed manner
- back out of a closed-off space
- walk over unusual surfaces
- walk through a curtain
- step into and out of a small space across a low barrier
- do all the above at a jog or trot

- do some of the above at a canter
- load into a trailer or truck, park in it, relaxed
- back out of a trailer or truck in a relaxed manner
- walk through tunnels
- walk through a narrow space with closed sides
- walk through a narrow space with spooky items on both sides.

Boots is trotting at liberty through a narrow lane of flags which was part of a Horse Agility course.

Goal Behavior:

The 'goal behavior' or 'complete task' is for the horse to lead politely beside the handler's shoulder, halt promptly, willingly walk forward on request, and back up straight, all with the horse and handler staying shoulder-to-shoulder. Once we have created these habits, the horse will be more comfortable and confident about walking with people.

Materials:

#39-#40 HorseGym with Boots illustrate the process.

- Work in an area where the horse feels comfortable. If possible, have his buddies in view but not able to interfere.
- Create a lane with sides about waist high so the rope easily floats over it, since the handler will be walking on the outside the lane while the horse is inside the lane.
- A lane could be made with a safe fence on one side and a rail sitting on two barrels or small jump stands forming the other side. The horse walks inside the lane. The handler walks on the outside of the lane.
- A marker and a mat a few meters out from either end of the lane can be used to change direction. The mat is closer to the end of the lane than the marker. The marker serves as a reference point around which to make a 180-degree U-turn.
- Two barrels are needed to create a dead end in the lane to aid in teaching the halt and the back-up. The lane in the video is about ten feet long and a bit more than three feet wide.

Method:

Slice 1: Walking confidently

Horse walks through the lane alongside the handler (who walks outside the lane) in both the left eye and the right eye.

We can walk a loop to return to the lane or set up two lanes and move from one to the other. Slices 2-4 below outline how to easily work on both sides of the horse with only one lane set up.

Slice 2: U-turn

Horse and handler make a U-turn around a marker, so facing the lane again, ready to head back into it. The U-turn might be rough at first, but with practice it will become tidier.

Slice 3: Mat

Horse targets his feet onto a mat and halts. The mat is set up between the U-turn marker and the end of the lane.

Slice 4: Changing eye

After the horse parks on the mat, the handler moves to the horse's other side. We are now in position to walk into the lane again, in the horse's other eye. This method of changing direction ensures we work equally on each side of the horse, helping the horse and the handler to become more ambidextrous.

Slice 5: Walk-on

'Walk-on' signal. We can teach this by walking the horse between nose targets or mats before getting to lane work. The 'go' button and the 'stop' button are the two signals that can make or break a lovely time with our horse, so it pays to take the time and effort to teach them well and generalize them to many situations.

The signals I use for 'Walk on' and 'Halt' are illustrated in *#17 HorseGym with Boots.*

Here is the signal bundle or multi-signal for 'walk-on'. We use the signals almost simultaneously:

- breathe in and raise body energy because horses are very conscious of when we breathe in deeply
- reach across with the *outside hand* and run it gently up the rope toward the halter
- step off with the outside leg - easier for horse to see
- say 'walk-on' (or whatever voice signal has been decided) because a voice signal is useful later when

working on a long line or guiding from behind, as in long-reining or liberty work

- apply energy behind with a body extension, but only if necessary and starting with a suggestion, then amplify slowly until the horse steps forward, at which point immediately put the body extension back into neutral. We can always bring it into play again if the horse hesitates again because he is unsure about what we want.

Slice 6: Halt

Our ideal is to get the 'whoa' to match the 'go'. If we lead the horse into a dead-end lane, it makes perfect sense to halt. If we click&treat every halt, we will build a strong history of reinforcement in the horse's mind. It's a good idea to build in a voice 'whoa' signal right from the beginning. There will be instances when a voice 'whoa' can keep us out of trouble.

Here is the signal bundle or multi-signal I use for the 'halt'. I use them almost simultaneously:

- visibly drop my weight down into my butt (like we want the horse to do)
- breathe out audibly
- say 'whoa' or whatever halt voice signal has been decided
- only if necessary, raise the inside hand holding the rope and jiggle the rope straight up and down. If we initially taught the halt signal and back up signals when the horse reached a corner or a fence (as in Training Plan Five), there will be less need to jiggle the rope or put energy out in front with a stick or string or rope.

The easiest way to teach the 'halt' is to ask for it as we walk the horse into a corner. It makes sense to the horse that he should halt. If the horse is already mat-savvy, we can use a mat in the corner at first. Once the corner halt is good, ask for a halt at the approach to a safe fence or barrier made with barrels or rails. Using a mat makes this task easier for a horse who already knows about targeting his front feet to a mat.

Slice 7 Back-Up out of a Lane

As mentioned earlier, *#39-#40 HorseGym with Boots* demonstrates the basic process.

#74 HorseGym with Boots goes through the process with a trailer simulation.

We can keep the horse's confidence and willingness by having the first lane-block near the entrance, so only a couple of steps back will have the horse out of the lane. Once the horse is halted facing the dead-end in the lane, it makes sense to him when we ask him to back out.

The barrel blocks off the lane. After we walk the horse into the lane, it makes sense to him when we ask him to back out of the lane because the way forward is blocked.

If the horse is new to this work, he may appreciate walking a loop away from the lane before entering it again and repeating the halt and the back-up. We want to avoid, at all costs, making him feel claustrophobic by going through these slices of behavior too fast. Depending on the nature of the horse and his past experiences, it can take ten minutes or weeks of short sessions to build confidence.

As the horse's confidence grows, block the lane further and further in until the horse is walking into the whole length of the lane and willingly backing all the way out on request. As mentioned above, it's good to vary how long we ask the horse to 'wait' at the halt before inviting him to back out.

Once a 10-second wait is solid, variation between 1 and 15-20 seconds is a good skill to develop. If we are working on pre-trailer loading skills, gradually achieving a relaxed wait time of 60 seconds is useful.

The clip, *#27 HorseGym with Boots* mentioned earlier, shows teaching the back-up in the horse's left eye. By using the other end of the lane, we can teach it again in the right eye. Regularly doing everything on both sides helps to consolidate the learning, generalize it, and put it into 'deep memory'.

In neurobiology, putting something into deep memory means we are thickening the myelin sheath around the nerve pathways that we are creating. The stronger the nerve pathway and its myelin sheath protection, the more established the behavior will become. It will become a habit. This also explains why habits are so hard to break.

Using a lane, during many short sessions over weeks, to play these sorts of 'lane games' is teaching the horse strong, positive habits. He will have more of the life skills he needs to get along in a human world.

Our final goal behavior is to have polite halts, leading and backing-up in many different environments. Rather than move 'cold turkey' out of our teaching laneway, it is helpful to gradually reduce the props in a way that lets the horse seamlessly move the habits learned in the lane to maintaining those habits all the time, anywhere.

In the 'Lanes' video clips, I laid another rail in front of the rail sitting on the barrels. That gave the horse a chest-high barrier on the far side, but only a ground rail between the handler and the horse. A set-up like this is good to check out whether the horse tends to push his shoulder into the handler — something that is common but not desirable.

If we've established a strong positive habit using the high-sided lane, the horse will usually stay straight. If he doesn't, we return to more sessions using the lane.

Whenever we make a significant change to a lane, it is important to review the training sequence again from the beginning:

- walk through both directions
- walk in, halt and walk on in both directions
- walk in, halt and back-up in both directions.

It's important that we don't presume the horse will be confident in any new lane we set up. It always pays to check it out carefully. When all the above slices are tidy, i.e, the horse remains straight, we can remove the ground rail and work with one high barrier on the far side of the horse, e.g. a fence.

If, at any time, the horse loses any of the skills, we simply go back to what we can do it easily and work forward again from there. It takes a fair amount of brief but consistent repetitions over many days to build a solid habit.

If the horse already has unwanted habits like pushing the shoulder into the handler, backing crooked, surging ahead or hanging behind during leading, it will take longer than if we are teaching a horse with none of those habits ingrained.

The goal behavior is to generalize the horse's confidence to work in all sorts of different lane set-ups and with the handler in different orientations and leading positions.

When the horse shows us that he is confident, we can use the lane to teach a variety of other moves, for example:

- send the horse into the lane on his own, as he would enter a horse trailer
- send the horse in, halt, ask him to back out with hand gesture signal
- send the horse through from leading position six (behind him) and follow him through
- all the above at liberty

- trot through — we can repeat all the lessons at trot.

Two rails lying on the ground is another form of laneway. The first step is to get the horse confident with the walk-through, halt halfway and walk-on forward, halt halfway and back out. We can repeat it all at trot if we are building the trot into our work. We can also add things like:

- Halt and back out with a tail signal from Leading Position Six (behind horse). #26 *HorseGym with Boots* describes the various leading positions.
- Walk horse into lane, turn to face him and ask him to back up using Leading Position Seven (in front, facing the horse) with rope-supported signals. This leading position is covered in *#41-#44 (inclusive) HorseGym with Boots*.
- Ask horse to back through the lane with gesture signals only.
- Walk into the lane in front of the horse, halt and ask him to back up with us remaining in Leading Position One (in front, facing away). This use a good skill for the horse to have if you navigate narrow trails or other narrow places where the horse walks behind you. *#45-#46 HorseGym with Boots* illustrates this.
- Lay unusual surfaces between the rails, e.g. mat or tarp or board. If the horse is already comfortable with walking on a tarp, we can set a rail lane on top of a tarp, or a tarp folded to fit inside the lane.

When we're ready, we can work with a single ground rail on the far side of the horse. Then we can work with a single ground rail between us and the horse. Once that is going smoothly, we have probably achieved our goal behavior — the creation of the habit of polite leading, halting and backing up in any situation.

The lane as an object to play with gives us the opportunity to engage in lots of different conversations.

Lanes don't have to be straight. They can be:

- L-bends
- U-bends create a nice flexion exercise.
- S-bends (two u-bends one after the other)
- zigzags.

Lanes can morph into other challenges, such as:

- bridges
- between vehicles
- narrow trails
- spooky corridors as in horse agility tunnels
- into horse trailers or trucks.

Confident trailer loading can start with the lane work outlined in Training Plan Eight.

Lanes can be usefully incorporated into a variety of Individual Education Programs (IEP)s. Often, they work as an excellent prop, allowing us to more easily clarify exactly what we would like the horse to do.

The longer we stay with a series of exercises, the more good things will begin happening. By 'longer', I mean doing a little bit over many, many sessions. It is never a matter of drilling something. As soon as there is improvement over last time, it's probably time to have a break by doing something else.

Once a desirable behavior has been formed into a strong habit, the horse will carry the habit with him into new situations. And we will have developed consistent habits about how we give the horse specific signals, how we read his responses and how we adjust our actions to suit the horse of the moment.

The lane prop will be a thing of the past unless we want to use it to help teach something new.

Playing at Liberty

Communicating with the horse at liberty tests the historical consistency and purity of our signals. In other words, how well have we taught the signals? Have we truly put them into the horse's deep memory? Are our signals clear and consistent?

When we use a halter and rope sympathetically, we are in essence 'holding hands' with the horse. The gear allows us to send a larger 'signal bundle'. The first step toward not needing the halter and rope is to have them on, but use the rope as little as possible.

In fact, it is often harder for the handler to 'let go' of the rope than it is for the horse to follow clear signals in the absence of the rope.

The key is to gradually transfer rope+halter-specific signals to voice and gesture signals. One by one, we replace each rope signal, fading out the need to use a rope to make that request. Switching to a light cord and using it as little as possible, seems to help both the horse and handler fade out reliance on rope signals.

Striving to keep a consistent 'smile' (drape) in the rope helps us learn to not use the rope at all. When the training is going well on a consistently draped rope, we can lay it over the horse's back at first, then take it off. Eventually we will feel confident to work without the halter as well. We can use a neck rope as an intermediary stage so we can supply extra support for something specific.

Boots is wearing a neck rope and a light cord lead so if we get confused, I can use them to clarify my meaning when we are working on a complex liberty Horse Agility course.

When we lose communication (notice, I said 'when' not 'if', because of course we will lose communication now and then) simply put some gear on again and backtrack in the Individual Education Program (IEP) to where the horse is confident. Then work forward again, tweaking the Program as needed.

For a horse who already knows about halters, I often use a system that moves through the following stages:

- halter and rope kept draped as much as possible
- halter and rope with the rope laid over the horse's back or around neck
- halter and light cord to keep draped
- halter and light cord with cord looped around neck
- neck rope with a light cord attached
- neck rope with the attached cord looped around neck
- neck rope only
- no gear on horse.

When the horse shows us that he is unsure about our intent, we smoothly and promptly return to providing more guidance. As long as we keep the horse's confidence uppermost, we'll be able to do more and more at liberty.

With clicker training, it is also possible to teach many things with the horse at liberty, then add the gear later.

My book, *Learn Universal Horse Language* sets out a series of activities all done at liberty in a roomy, enclosed area. The information applies to any horse, young or old, new or long-time friend. It is designed to establish ease and confidence being with a horse at liberty.

Using clicker training, we can free-shape many behaviors without using a halter and lead. Once the horse understands targeting (with nose and feet) we can teach leading positions, backing up, moving independently between targets, and so on, without the need for a rope.

In other words, we teach what we want at liberty, and then add the halter and rope/rein signals in order to make the horse comfortable wearing the gear he needs to be safe away from home.

#83 and #84 HorseGym with Boots illustrates ways to have fun teaching the horse to move with us willingly at liberty.

A Few More Snippets

** Learning something new and meaningful requires a lot of mental, physical and emotional energy, especially when first getting started. There are no short cuts.

** We need to appreciate that everything the horse does in our company is feedback. Feedback can be positive, negative or neutral and all of it has the same value.

** Horses can perceive us either as predators, something to be eternally wary of, or as part of their personal herd - maybe even a best buddy.

** Once we learn to read our horse's body language, we will know when he is approaching the edge of his comfort zone. That allows us to adjust what we do in order to retain his confidence rather than lose it.

** Sometimes we are so used to doing or seeing something done, that we seldom stop to think about it, e.g. horses wearing bits, tight nosebands, steel shoes nailed into living tissue, horses in winter covers on a hot sunny day, horses kept in boxes like chocolates.

** Relationships with horses, just like person-person relationships, can only grow and develop through time spent together doing enjoyable things.

** Every moment we spend with a horse is different. There is never a time when we stop reading the horse and adjusting our responses and requests.

** Horses don't do things to annoy us. At any moment in time the horse is doing what he believes is the best thing to do to keep himself safe or amused.

** The process of teaching does not look like the finished product.

Rainy Day or Stall Rest Clicker Games

We can teach these using finesse rope handling skills and then move to playing with the horse at liberty. Or we can teach them with the horse at liberty.

If the horse is recovering from injury, hopefully he can still do some of these.

1. Head down & head up standing on left & right (See *Free-Shaping* clips called *'Head Lowering'* – 2 clips)
2. Willing haltering *(#65 HorseGym with Boots)*
3. Lateral flexion of neck to touch a hand-held target - right and left (See *#2 HorseGym with Boots* and *#32* for this and no. 3. below)
4. Vertical flexion to a target held between the front legs, standing on left & right
5. Nose to target high, low, right & left (See *#2 HorseGym with Boots* and *'Introducing Smoky to the Nose Target'* in the *Free-Shaping* Playlist)
6. Target left front knee to object or hand (See *#32 HorseGym with Boots* for activities 5. to 15.)
7. Target right front knee to object or hand
8. Target ear to hand (right and left ears)
9. Target chin to hand, standing on right and left sides
10. Target shoulder to hand, right & left sides
11. Target ribs to hand, right & left sides
12. Target hip to hand, right & left sides
13. Back up with signal from behind – tail signal & gesture signal, from right & left sides of horse
14. Turn on forequarters right & left
15. Turn on hindquarters right & left (See also *'Shoulder Yield into a Turn on the Haunches'* in the *Thin-Slicing* Playlist)
16. Belly crunches

17. Head rocking (See two *'Head Rocking'* clips in the *Thin-Slicing* Playlist)
18. Pick up objects (See two clips about Smoky and Boots learning to pick up a dumb-bell in the *Free-Shaping* Playlist)
19. Lift hind foot on signal, right and left sides
20. Back leg stretches – out behind and bring forward, left and right sides
21. In-Hand Back Up (See *#27 HorseGym with Boots*)
22. Backing corners from the right side and the left side
23. Back 2-3 steps & recall 2-3 steps (See the *'The Box' Movement* in the *Thin-Slicing* Playlist for activities 22. to 25.)
24. Sideways away 2-3 steps to the right & to the left
25. Sideways toward 2-3 steps to the right and to the left
26. Square dance: back 2-3 steps, sideways 2-3 steps, recall 2-3 steps and sideways 2-3 steps
27. Soft yield to the rope or rein (See the five clips on this topic in the *Thin-Slicing* Playlist)

List of YouTube Video Clips

Most of the video clips are shorter than five minutes, so they are quick to watch and easy to review if you are interested in specific tasks.

To reach my channel, put *Hertha MuddyHorse* into the YouTube search engine. The Clips are in one of three playlists.

1. Most of the clips are in my *HorseGym with Boots* playlist. Each title is written as #__ *HorseGym with Boots*. For example, if you want to quickly find Clip number 22, simply put: *#22 HorseGym with Boots* into the YouTube search engine and it should come right up.
2. Some clips are in the *Free-Shaping Examples* playlist. These are named only, so to find a particular clip, go to that playlist and scroll down for the clip's name.
3. Other clips are in the *Thin-Slicing Examples* playlist. These are also only named, so you search the playlist for the title you want.

A list of all the current *HorseGym with Boots* Clips follows, as well as titles in the *Free-Shaping* and *Thin-Slicing* examples.

HorseGym with Boots Series

Topics are added to this series as they are created.

1. Introduction
2. Giving meaning to the click
3. Stationary nose targets
4. Parking at a nose target (also spooky new things to touch)
5. Putting behavior 'on cue'

6. Foot targets (also, free-shaping new behavior)
7. Backing up from the mat
8. Duration on the mat
9. Putting the mat target 'on cue'
10. Generalizing mats
11. Mat-a-thons
12. Chaining tasks
13. Anthem is new to nose targets (Anthem is a young quarter-horse)
14. Anthem is new to foot targets
15. Parking at a distance
16. The 'triple treat'
17. 'Walk-on' and 'halt' multi-cues
18. Parking out of sight
19. Free-shaping
20. The 'art of standing still'
21. Walk away for confidence (with new things)
22. Rope relaxation
23. Hosing on the mat (recognizing 'click points')
24. Parking commotions
25. Parking with ball commotion
26. 8 Leading Positions overview
27. Good Backing = Good Leading
28. Leading Position Three (beside neck or shoulder)
29. Leading Position Three with a 'circle of markers'
30. Leading Position Three duration exercise
31. Natural and Educated body language signals
32. Sensitivity to Body language
33. Opportunity, Signals 1
34. Signals 2: Gestures
35. Signals 3: Touch
36. Signals 4: Verbal signals (also environmental signals, horse initiated signals and marker signals)
37. Signals 5: Intent
38. Signals 6: Body Orientation (of handler)
39. Train with a Lane 1
40. Train with a Lane 2
41. Leading Position Seven Clip 1 of 4, in front facing horse

42. Leading Position Seven Clip 2 of 4
43. Leading Position Seven Clip 3 of 4
44. Leading Position Seven Clip 4 of 4
45. Leading Position One: Clip 1 of 2 in front, facing away
46. Leading Position One Clip 2 of 2
47. Leading Position Two (horse's nose stays behind handler's shoulder)
48. Leading Position Eight Clip 1 of 7, Go, Whoa & Back (facing the horse's side)
49. Leading Position Eight Clip 2 of 7, Groom, Saddle, Relax
50. Leading Position Eight Clip 3 of 7, Drive-by Grooming & Mounting Prep
51. Leading Position Eight Clip 4 of 7, Side Step in Motion
52. Leading Position Eight Clip 5 of 7, Yielding Front End & Hind End
53. Leading Position Eight Clip 6 of 7, Side Step from Halt
54. Leading Position Eight Clip 7 of 7, Arc Exercise
55. Leading Positions Four and Five (beside ribs & beside butt)
56. Leading Position Four, Clip 2
57. Leading Position Six Clip 1 of 8, Liberty (behind horse)
58. Leading Position Six Clip 2 of 8, One long rein
59. Leading Position Six Clip 3 of 8, Square of lanes
60. Leading Position Six Clip 4 of 8, Rope Calmness
61. Leading Position Six Clip 5 of 8, Two Long Reins: Circle & Weaving
62. Leading Position Six Clip 6 of 8, 4 Leaf Clover Exercise
63. Leading Position Six Clip 7 of 8, 'Gates', Guided Rein, Obstacles
64. Leading Position Six Clip 8 of 8, Trailer Prep
65. Haltering process (with guided free-shaping)
66. Importance of Clear Signals
67. Prep 1 for Weaving, 90 and 180 degree turns; 'Draw' and 'Drive'

68. Weave Prep 2, 360 degree turns
69. Weave Prep 3, Weave a series of objects
70. Weave Prep 4, Only the horse weaves
71. Weave Prep 5, Curves, Circles, at Liberty
72. Ground-tie Clip 1, Getting Started
73. Ground-tie Clip 2, Another Venue
74. Thin-slicing a Trailer Simulation
75. Quiet Sharing of Time and Place
76. Active Sharing of Time and Place + Greet & Go
77. Claim the Spot
78. Watchfulness First Action
79. Watchfulness Second & Third Actions
80. Guiding from Behind
81. Shadow Me
82. Boomerang Frolic
83. Shadow Me Duration with Clicker Training
84. Shadow Me Using Targets

Thin-Slicing Examples

This playlist includes thin-slicing examples about the following topics. To find a specific clip, go to the *Thin-Slicing Examples* playlist in my channel and scroll down to find the one you want. New clips are added as they are made.

- Tunnel with Boots
- Pool Noodle task
- Head Rocking for Poll Relaxation
- Bottle Bank obstacle
- Zigzag for Horse Agility
- Yield Shoulder into a Turn on the Haunches
- Stepping over rails
- Soft yield to Rein Signals (5 Clips which also have their own Playlist)
- Thin-slice '*The Box*' Movement (back, sideways, forward, sideways)
- Backing up
- Rope Texting
- Thin-slicing the 1m board

- Water & Tarp obstacle
- Thin-slice the 'Shadow Me' Game at Liberty
- Free-shape Learning to Ring a Bell

Free-Shaping Examples

This playlist includes clips using the free-shaping technique to teach a task. To find a particular clip, go to the *Free-Shaping Examples* playlist in my channel and scroll down to find the clip you want. Most of these clips show both free-shaping and thin-slicing.

- Table Manners for Clicker Training
- Boots and Bicycle
- Bob meets Bicycle (Bob is a young quarter horse)
- Introduction to a saddle (with Bob, his first meeting with a saddle)
- Head-lowering (2 Clips)
- Clicker 1 with Smoky
- Smoky and Dumb-bell target
- Boots picks up the Dumb-bell
- Free-shape Learning to Ring a Bell

There are also short playlists on specific topics including:

- Thin-slicing the Wagon-wheel obstacle
- Teaching the S-bend
- Soft Yield to Rein Signals (5 clips)
- Hula Hoop Challenges (5 clips)
- Single Obstacle Challenges
- 2012 Horse Agility
- 2014 Horse Agility
- 2015 Horse Agility
- 2016 Horse Agility

Most of the Horse Agility clips have a commentary explaining the tasks and showing where we lost marks. Each task is marked out of ten, five points for the handler and five points for the horse. Some are at liberty and others are with halter and lead. Horse Agility is at www.thehorseagilityclub.com.

Further Resources Available from the Author:

Hard Copy Book:

Natural Horsemanship Study Guide

Available by contacting me at: <u>hertha.james@xtra.co.nz</u>.

Natural Horsemanship Study Guide. (2012). Powerword Publications; Palmerston North, NZ. The Book is in 2 volumes, over 400 pages, well-illustrated, indexed, referenced, supported with three DVDs.

This book brings together the philosophy and basic methodology of the worldwide movement called Natural Horsemanship. It looks in detail at ground work up to and including trailer loading, saddling and unsaddling.

The underlying aim of Natural Horsemanship is to teach us to work with the horse's nature rather than struggle against it.

The book is presented in two volumes so that it is easy to cross-reference the lesson plans in Volume 2 with the extensive information in Volume 1. It is a hands-on study guide complete with:

- a glossary with detailed notes covering key words and concepts
- a step-by-step guide to learning *International Horse Language*, all done at liberty
- outlines to help you get good at 'reading your horse'
- practical exercises toward smooth gear handling
- goal setting and easy recording of your progress
- guidelines to help create good lesson plans for any specific horse
- clear, detailed information showing you how to teach your horse nine basic ground moves, polite saddling, drive-by grooming and trailer-loading.
- sequential lesson plans including written tasks to speed up learning of concepts and terminology, as well as practical tasks to develop your skills.

DVD & Notes Sets:

Available by contacting me at hertha.james@xtra.co.nz.

Teaching Long-Reining with Positive Reinforcement

This DVD and 26-page booklet breaks long-reining into its smallest teachable parts. Then it shows Smoky going through the initial learning process and Boots demonstrating some of the finer points.

Harness Horse/Pony Preparation using Positive Reinforcement

This DVD and 23-page booklet go through the stages of developing a horse's confidence to wear harness, hitch up and pull a cart at home in a controlled situation.

My Other Books Available from Amazon.com.

You can find these books any time by putting my name (Hertha James) into the Amazon search engine. A short review on Amazon is always appreciated.

- *Conversations with Horses: An In-depth look at the Signals & Cues between Horses and their Handlers*
- *Walking with Horses: The Eight Leading Positions*
- *Learn Universal Horse Language: No Ropes*
- *How to Create Good Horse Training Plans: The Art of Thin-Slicing*

If you prefer e-books but don't have a Kindle reader, Amazon has a free Kindle reader which can be downloaded to any computer, tablet or smartphone.

Reference List

Resources Specifically about Positive Reinforcement Training, Clicker Training or Mark & Reward Training

Abrantes, Roger. DVDs (2013). *The 20 Principles all Animal Trainers Must Know.* Tawzer Dog LLC. www.TawzerDog.com

Bailey, Nancy J. *15 Rules of Clicker training Your Horse.* (Kindle e-book; www.amazon.com.)

Camp, Joe (2011). Training with Treats: with relationship & basic training locked in, treats can become an excellent way to enhance good communication. 14 Hands Press; USA.

Foley, Sharon. (2007). *Getting to Yes: Clicker training for improved horsemanship.* T.F.H. Publications Inc.; Neptune City, NJ, USA.

Freeman, Kim. (2012). Clicker training Fun with Horses: quick tips to improve your results & relationship with your horse. (Kindle e-book; www.amazon.com.)

Hanson, Mark. (2011). *Revealing Your Hidden Horse: a revolutionary approach to understanding your horse.* (Amazon On-Demand Publishing; www.amazon.com.)

Hart, Ben. (2008). *The Art and Science of Clicker training for Horses.* Souvenir Press Ltd; London. (Kindle e-book; www.amazon.com.)

Karrasch, Shawna. (2012). *You Can Train Your Horse to do Anything! On Target™ Training: Clicker training and Beyond.* (Amazon On-Demand Publishing; www.amazon.com.)

Kurland, Alexandra. (2005). *The Click That Teaches; riding with the clicker.* The Clicker Center; Delmar, New York.

MacLeay, Jennifer. (2003). *Smart Horse: understanding the science of natural horsemanship.* Blood Horse Publications; Lexington, Ky.

Minden, Cynthia. (2015). *A Donkey Diary: One Click, One Treat: why I prefer this approach to positive reinforcement* training. Blog Post Sep 2015Nellist, Jenni. (2014) Clicker training for Horses: foundation lessons; Swansea; UK. (Kindle e-book; www.amazon.com.)

Pavlich, Leslie. (2008). *Clicker training: Colt Starting the Natural Horse.* (Amazon On-Demand Publishing; www.amazon.com.)

Pryor, Karen. (1999). *Don't Shoot the Dog: the new art of teaching and training.* Bantam; New York. {About much more than dogs.}

Pryor, Karen. (2009). *Reaching the Animal Mind: Clicker training and what it teaches us about all animals.* Scribner; New York.

Pryor, Karen. (2014). *On My Mind: reflections on animal behavior and learning.* Sunshine Books Inc.; Waltham, MA, USA.

Schneider, Susan M. (2012). *The Science of Consequences: how they affect genes, change the brain and impact our world.* Prometheus Books; New York.

General Books About Getting Along with Horses

Budiansky, Stephen. (1997). *The Nature of the Horse: Their Evolution, Intelligence and Behavior.* Phoenix; London.

Burns, Stephanie. (2002). *Move Closer Stay Longer.* Parelli Natural Horsemanship; Pagosa Springs, Colorado.

Dorrance, Bill & Desmond, Leslie. (2001). *True Horsemanship Through Feel.* First Lyons Press; Guilford, CT.

Miller, Dr Robert M. (1999). *Understanding the Ancient Secrets of the Horse's Mind.* The Russell Meerdink Co. Ltd.; Neenah, WI, USA.

Resnick, Carolyn. (2005). *Naked Liberty: Memoirs of my Childhood: the language of movement, communication, and leadership through the way of horses.* Amigo Publications; Los Olivos, CA.

Hertha James

Tiakitahuna, New Zealand

2017

hertha.james@xtra.co.nz

www.safehorse.info

www.herthamuddyhorse.com